The Seven
Secrets
of
Greatness

"How to discover your true purpose,
find your power & achieve the impossible."

ADAM
YANNOTTA

YANNOTTA, ADAM, Author
THE & SECRETS OF GREATNESS

Published by:
ELITE ONLINE PUBLISHING
63 East 11400 South
Suite #230
Sandy, UT 84070
EliteOnlinePublishing.com

ISBN: 978-1-961801-33-2
ISBN: 978-1-961801-34-9

SEL027000
BUS107000

QUANTITY PURCHASES: Schools, companies, professional groups, clubs, and other organizations may qualify for special terms when ordering quantities of this title. For information, email info@eliteonlinepublishing.com.

For updates and more visit
7secrets.us2.authorhomepage.com

Table of Contents

Foreword

As someone who's been channeling metaphysical information to the public for over forty years, I've come to appreciate when a person like Adam not only has a solid grasp of the fundamentals, but can express the principles in ways that provide practical explanations of the topic that, when applied to everyday situations, can greatly improve people's daily lives.

To me, this is a very important service to humanity because many metaphysical and spiritual subjects often remain esoteric and easily misunderstood. By presenting a clear understanding of these concepts in this breakthrough book, Adam not only creates a guide for how to live a more fulfilled life, but also offers a foundation for the further exploration of metaphysics, as well as demonstrating that physical reality and spiritual awareness can enhance each other in profoundly powerful ways.

For anyone passionate about metaphysics, or even simply curious about how to allow more spiritual awareness and creativity into their lives, this book can serve as a doorway to a bigger world.

Darryl Anka
Channel for "Bashar"

Introduction

It's the things that we understand the least,
where the answers may lie.

A re you in debt? Are you unsatisfied with your work? Do you feel like your purpose is meant for something bigger? If so, you're in the right place.

You see, each and every one of us has a power so unique, so magnificent, that once we discover it, we not only escape "the matrix," we become a master of It. This book will show you how, but before that's possible, you may have to challenge what you believe to be true regarding outdated paths to success, which may do more to enslave than empower you.

I used to believe in those paths too. I was taught to work hard, get good grades, earn a scholarship, go to a good college, study hard, earn a degree, get a job at a reputable corporation, work my way up to the top of the ladder, and hopefully after 20–30 years of hard work, I'd be able to achieve some form of career fulfillment or financial independence. Eventually, I realized that's not success—it's failure.

Whether through accumulating massive amounts of debt to pay for college, or by simply trying to live The American Dream, we become slaves to the system. We are programmed to fail. This programming sucks the creative life out of all those who travel these outdated paths, and our initial intention of success is replaced with an objective to survive.

Imagine discovering the secret to creating the life of your dreams. After stepping off the path I'd been following, I vowed that I would find the secret of success, and once I did, I would teach it to the masses. Over my twenty-five-year journey to find this "recipe," I learned lessons from some of the greatest minds of the past two millennia, and—I couldn't believe it—the same principles kept repeating.

How could no one have discovered these secrets? I wondered. *Why has this ancient well of knowledge been hidden from humanity? Why aren't we shouting these secrets from the mountaintops?* I have my guesses, but no longer can these secrets remain hidden. It's time for us to reclaim our true power.

This book details the Seven Secrets I learned and acts as an instruction manual for implementing them, guiding you each step of the way. Life can be brutal, but this book will show you how to master it!

How I Discovered the Seven Secrets

Deep down, I knew that almost everything I learned in school and much of what I was being taught about success didn't feel right, but as a lifelong student of human behavior, I played along anyway. I've always been interested in the potential that exists in all of us, so I observed and recorded each step along the way.

However, my own life was an amalgamation of physical, emotional, and financial stress. As the owner of a multi-million-dollar real estate business, I had to balance millions worth of debt and leverage, which sucked the life out of me. I was also married, raising a family, expanding my business, and paying for advanced degrees.

I thought that success equals happiness, so I began feverishly studying timeless personal empowerment masterpieces from extraordinary people, such as Napoleon Hill, Dale Carnegie, Anthony Robbins, and Stephen Covey. I immersed myself in many books encompassing The Law of Attraction, especially *The Secret* by Rhonda Byrne. I read many spiritual and ancient texts, including the Bible, the Bhagavad Gita, the Ramayana, the Nag Hammadi scriptures, The Emerald Tablets, and The Kybalion. I engrossed myself in the lives and lessons of people who have changed the course of history, such as Cyrus the Great, Socrates, Plato, Aristotle, Alexander the Great, and Julius Caesar.

What I found was something better, something more relevant—and even more practical—than a recipe for success.

I learned that success is the wrong term to use. **The term that embodies total success is FULFILLMENT.** Who cares if you're successful if you're not fulfilled? Some of the most successful people in the world—actors, musicians, business leaders, reality stars, even billionaires—are no happier than someone living in an igloo in the North Pole. Why? How can that be? From my experience, success doesn't always translate to happiness, but fulfillment does. Fulfillment is true happiness, and it's achieved not with success, not with material goods, not with fame and fortune, but with a knowingness that you are the creator of your own reality, and your imagination is the bridge that connects you to your greatest life.

I learned that money comes and goes, but wisdom remains. Wisdom is power. Wisdom is abundance. Wisdom is knowledge gained through experience. Wisdom is a deeply ingrained emotional and spiritual knowingness. Wisdom is nourishment for the soul. Wisdom is what separates one who is fulfilled in life and one who is always looking for something more. Wisdom is the pathway to our greatest self!

I learned Universal laws—what I call the Seven Secrets—that, when applied, changed my life, seemingly overnight. I became debt-free, digging myself out of a 5-million-dollar hole, and was able to retire from my 9–5 day job while maintaining total financial independence.

You must be reading this, saying, "Did a rich relative die or something? Did you win the lottery? Are you making this up?" At least, that's what I'd have said after reading this type of testimonial. When I was $5 million in debt, I would have thrown this book across the room out of frustration. But now I know that, if you learn and apply these Seven Secrets, you too will acquire the tools and techniques needed to escape the rat race.

My goal is to help you exit "the matrix" so that you have the time and freedom to create something that will make this world a better place for all of us—or, at the very least, so that you can become an example for others to follow. This is how we change the world.

In this book, you will learn that you do not have to work harder, you do not have to apply complex strategies in your life, you don't have to go back to school, nor do you have to get a high-paying job. In fact, you do not have to do anything different but relax, because everything in our lives is and has always been moving in the right direction, and the only thing we need to do is lighten up and get out of our own way so ideas, inspirations, and insights can emerge. It's up to us to act on the ideas, inspirations, and insights that excite us the most; in doing so, we are led to our greatest path, our greatest self, and our greatest life!

This is not theory; this is not observation. It's simply physics. What we put out in this world we get back, what we think about regularly we attract more of, what we act on we create more of, and what we believe to be true will be reflected to us in physical reality.

Tapping into the Field of Infinite Knowledge

There is one amazing, extraordinary aspect of human potential that seems to contain all the answers to all the secrets, as well as all the knowledge and all the wisdom necessary for an individual to master their own life and for humanity to flourish in general. Very few people have been able to tap into this infinite knowledge bank, but those who do push the limits of human potential beyond the impossible.

This next level of human development revolves around accessing higher levels of consciousness and thought so we can break from the matrix programming that has many of us trapped in a prison of our own making.

Humanity is at the beginning stages of neuroscience, and it would be irresponsible for me to say that I completely understand the true potential and dynamics of the conscious and unconscious mind. However, what I lack in knowledge on this subject I make up with the first-hand experience of someone who is able to get into a meditative, hypnotic state and access the seemingly infinite amount of knowledge and information offered by the *higher mind*.

Sometimes in life, there's a person that we meet—whether it's a teacher, a mentor, or a friend—who by the grace of God helps us to find something in us that we never knew we had. They enable us to change our life, take control of our destiny, and become the person we were truly meant to be.

For me, that person is Darryl Anka, known for being **THE** best channeler in the world today and one of the most fascinating individuals I've worked with or studied in my life. Using the power of the higher mind Darryl gets himself into a hypnotic state, similar to Edgar Cayce (the sleeping prophet) or Nostradamus (a world-renowned sixteenth-century physician and astrologer, who would gaze into the flame of a lit candle and see prophetic visions). It's in this semi-sleep but hyper-focused channeling state, that Darryl is able to shut off his physical mind and access this infinite field of knowledge. As he does, some of the most beautiful, life-changing information is spoken to all who are fortunate enough to hear him. This book contains much of the knowledge I've gathered from many different private sessions with Darryl; he is the creator of what I refer to as Secret #7: The Formula, and many of his teachings can be found in Secrets #1–6.

It's okay if you're skeptical; I was too. This book may challenge your ideas and beliefs regarding human potential, but if you put your skepticism aside, the Seven Secrets are worth it.

In fact, one of the first questions I asked Darryl was about how it could be possible for a human to speak on such complex topics without pausing or without flubbing a word, and to do it so clearly that all could understand. It's mind-blowing to me because he does things linguistically that defy human capabilities.

The documentary *First Contact* shows how Darryl had once gone for an EEG (electroencephalogram), which is a brain wave analysis test. It monitored his brain's electrical activity while he was in the channeling state. **Below are the results.**

Analysis by Dr. Jeannine Lemare Calaba, Clinical Psychologist:

So, in the channeling state, Darryl experiences changes in the brain that, statistically, less than 1% of the population would experience in the same way. He increases his processing speed, he tunes it exquisitely to 1 frequency all over the brain, and then he's able to create a resonant holding environment for the peak performance or the channeling to happen. He pumps energy into the right frontal cortex and the right auditory cortex so that he can empathize and hear very, very, clearly, and because of the gamma frequencies in the anterior cingulate, he can shift gears and navigate cognition, thoughts, and emotions very flexibly, and he'll be able to interpret from a higher perspective, from a more evolved place in his mind, much like from the highest mountain top.[i]

Darryl connects telepathically to what he describes as a separate extra-terrestrial entity named Bashar (Bashar = The Messenger in Arabic), so for the rest of the book, I will refer to Darryl as Bashar. If this seems far-fetched, you should know that Socrates, the founder of Western philosophy, had also attributed his knowledge to a separate entity he communicated with. He referred to this as a divine inner voice that he believed was a gift from the gods. He named it his "Daimon."

Whether consciously or unconsciously, the Seven Secrets outlined in this book have been used by the most accomplished people in the history of known humanity, from the most well-known philosophers and successful army generals in antiquity to the greatest athletes and minds today. The best part about tapping into this wealth of knowledge is that you don't need to be hypnotized; you don't need to do anything except be in the right state of being, which will attract to you all the knowledge and information necessary for you to master life. This book shows you how to get into this peak state so that you begin to operate on the level of a true life master.

Important Terms

Consciousness is the unique awareness of our thoughts, feelings, emotions, surroundings, and perceptions in physical reality. It's our ability to observe, take note of, integrate, process, and make use of both the seen and the unseen, the known and the unknown, the probable and the improbable, the possible and the impossible.

Synchronicity is the simultaneous occurrence of events that appear significantly related but have no discernible connection. Have you ever been in the right place at the right time? That wasn't luck; it wasn't by accident. There are no accidents—our entire lives have been carefully synchronized and orchestrated in such a manner that is more perfect than we could imagine.

The Universe is the almighty intelligence conducting the laws and principles of existence! Other names for this supreme power are God, Creator, Source, All-Knowing, All-Powerful, All That Is.

The higher mind acts as a satellite connecting "the Universe" and all its intelligence to our physical mind. The "higher mind" may be able to provide us with all the answers to all the questions to all the mysteries, possibilities, and wonders creation has to offer. How exciting is that?

"The higher mind can see the past, present, and future like a film reel. The limited physical mind cannot see the entire picture. If we put our trust in the higher mind, we can relax our physical mind and allow life-changing ideas, inspirations, and insights to filter through."

–Bashar

The physical mind is made up of three components: the *unconscious*, the *subconscious*, and the *conscious*.

1. Think of the *unconscious mind* as an antenna that receives wonderful, life-changing information and insights from the higher mind, and then delivers that information to the *subconscious mind*.

2. Think of the *subconscious mind* as a "gatekeeper" allowing only the prescreened concepts to filter down from the *unconscious mind* to the *conscious mind*.

Why is this important? The *subconscious mind* will filter down information and insights based on the beliefs and programming you bought into in this lifetime. This is one of the main reasons people fail continuously. If you already bought into limiting beliefs like "I'm not good enough," "There's no point in trying," "The system is rigged," or "Money is evil," the *subconscious mind* will filter away the ideas, insights, and information that would have supported instead of hindered you on your path to greatness.

3. The *conscious mind* is a composite of our thoughts, actions, and awareness of physical reality.

The Matrix is a controlled simulation that is fueled by the energy and emotions of those who cannot access higher levels of consciousness and thought.

"There are powers that be" which deploy many different tactics to keep humanity mired in an unconscious state so that we don't question nor threaten the "Matrix" simulation. Education, movies, music, news media, and now social media, with its advanced mind-control algorithms, work together like never before to keep us trapped in a never-ending cycle of work, spending, debt, and stress loops. This prevents us from accessing the power of higher creative thought, cutting us off from the ideas and insights that will help us break free from these cycles.

If we can't see, touch, taste, smell, hear, or physically prove "something," then it's hard to believe that "something" exists; however, those who *cannot* access higher levels of consciousness and thought, beyond the five senses, will become the workers and servants for those who can.

The secrets in this book will show you how to tap into a higher power so you can break free from the programming and live your greatest life.

Are you ready to learn the Seven Secrets? Are you ready to become the person you are truly meant to be, so you can live the life you are truly meant to live?

One thing is for certain: we are more special and much more powerful than we think! This is the next level of human achievement.

Secret #1:
Miracles Are the Norm

If you feel like you don't belong in this world, maybe you don't!
Maybe you're not "here" to "belong" in this world!
Maybe you're "here" to change it!

At some point, I began noticing strange things happening more and more in my life. Whenever the thought of a repeating number popped into my head, I would look at the clock and see 11:11 or 12:12 or 1:11 or 2:22. Or I would say an unusual word only to hear that exact same word being said on the television at the exact same time. It started with small miracles occurring here and there, but it gradually increased to incredible coincidences and synchronicities that left me dumbfounded.

One experience was so unbelievable that I felt I couldn't tell anyone about it. I almost couldn't believe it myself.

Walking in nature is one of the most effective things we can do to connect to our hidden power, so I make it a point to get out as often as possible. While on walks, ideas flow through me like a waterfall dancing down the side of a mountain. To maximize my chances of inspiration, I listen to all different kinds of audiobooks or podcasts, and on this occasion, I just so happened to be listening to a previous recording from one of Bashar's magnificent in-person events.

During my walk, while listening to the event, I heard an audience member ask a question about crystals. I am unsure what else was said because for some reason my shoelace was starting to become untied. I bent down to tie my shoe, and—I kid you not—I found a large amethyst crystal right next to my foot. I picked up the purple rock, put it in my pocket, and felt an infusion of energy in every cell in my body, awakening me to the realization that there is way more to life than what we can see with our eyes. This wasn't my first miracle, but it was this time that I asked, "How can something like this even happen? Has the Universe singled me out?"

The truth is that the Universe does this for everyone and for anyone who can recognize that there is an unseen force that guides all things. Some call this force God, others call it "the Universe," or "All That Is," but whatever this force of nature is, once you tap into it, miracles become the norm in life, not the exception. Who would ever have guessed that a few years later I'd be writing a book with the help of the same person I was listening to the moment I found that crystal?

This unseen force cleverly gives us what we need in life and not necessarily what we want. It understands that we change and grow as unique individuals, and as soon as we become the person we are truly meant to be, as soon as our needs become our wants, this force seems to go out of its way to grant us whatever our heart desires. Like a loving parent, this force allows us to make mistakes and learn on our own, but it will never leave us, it will never abandon us, and if we tap into it, it will guide us to our greatest life.

The most successful people in the world throughout history have figured this out. Thomas Edison, Andrew Carnegie, and Dr. Alexander Graham Bell went as far as contributing much of their success to an unseen force that guided them in their quest and desire to achieve the impossible. Dr. Bell believed this invisible force was in direct contact with "infinite intelligence."[ii]

Discovering this force is of the utmost importance because it's the first step in becoming the person we are truly meant to be. It's why certain people accomplish the impossible while others stay in a state of fear and comfort! When we claim this power, the things that no longer serve us—whether they're negative people in our lives or careers we are no longer passionate about—become more evident. Once we shed the weight of that which no longer serves us, we feel lighter, more energetic, and happier.

People will notice a change in you; they will wonder what has happened to you. You may begin to attract the people in your life who have also discovered this force, as well as opportunities, abundance, and prosperity. Like a snowball rolling down a hill, your miracles may grow in size, strength, and speed as time goes by.

The goal of Secret #1 is to recognize that this miracle force exists, to tap into this magic, and allow it to guide you on your greatest path!

This force guides us by way of synchronicity and coincidence, and the more we look out of it, the more it makes itself known to us. It has always been guiding us, sometimes even breaking us down, not to hurt us but to help us become the person we are truly meant to be. Sometimes it's in the state of suffering where we finally discover this force, but as soon as we do, life becomes magical!

Once we discover this Secret, there is no limit to how great our lives can be. Some may doubt this phenomenon, as I did myself, especially early on, but there comes a time when it becomes mathematically impossible to see so many miracles each day. This miracle force exists, and as soon as we begin to acknowledge it, our lives—which were previously mired in challenge and struggle—become full of joy and excitement, because we now know that we are guided and protected each step of the way.

Our Imagination is The Key That Opens the Door to Our Greatest Life

You are unlike any person in the world. Your successes and your failures, your trials and tribulations, your thoughts and ideas, they are so unique that there is no one exactly like you in the Universe. You are part of this amazing creation we call life, and "all of creation" could not be "all of creation" without you.

Since you are part of this wonderful creation, what could you do to make all of creation better? In other words, what can you create? No one thinks exactly like you; no one has had the same experiences as you; no one has lived your life. Only you can think of your idea and use all of your specific talents and experiences to bring it to life. Each person has a thought, a song, or a book that can change the world, but to access these ideas, you have to THINK.

Some of the best ways to promote thinking:

1. **Meditation:** Meditation techniques can be as simple as shutting off your thoughts by closing your eyes and concentrating on your breath. Relax the jaw, then inhale through your nose and feel the breath relax every cell in the body, and exhale through the mouth and allow it to relax you even more. Just a few minutes of breathwork can eliminate years of neurological programming. Meditation seems to rewire the brain circuitry, so our thoughts, behaviors, and actions change.

   When I first began meditating, I noticed my food preference changed, as did my music preference. My ability to focus greatly increased and I began to think differently. I literally became a new person, and this inevitably allowed me to solve problems in my life by looking at them from a different point of view.

Other forms of meditation can be as simple as taking a walk in nature, painting a picture, sitting in silence pondering ideas, or maybe sitting on a beach, becoming aware of the waves as they dance in and out.

2. **Channeling State:** The channeling state is a meditative state, but the difference is that instead of shutting your thoughts off, you allow ideas, thoughts, visions, and inspirations to flow into your mind while you're relaxed.

   You can get yourself in the channeling state by simply doing what you love to do, such as reading, writing, or listening to an audiobook. Some get into this state while playing the piano or writing music. Some get into this state while driving or taking a shower. There are no rules for getting into this peak mental state, but once you do, be ready for the Universe to communicate with you. Once you are inspired, it's up to you to act!

The imagination is a divine antenna that receives waves of information flowing through our cosmic reality. When we meditate, get into the channeling state, or access our imagination in any way, even when we're daydreaming, hours pass by in what feels like minutes. In this state, people forget who they are and what they are, and before they realize it, they discover a cure for a disease or solve a mathematical equation that has life-changing consequences for humanity. In this state, people can seemingly achieve the impossible or even predict the future.

"Bohemian Rhapsody" is an example of how the channeling state might cause someone to unknowingly predict the future. Written and sung by Freddie Mercury of the band Queen, "Bohemian Rhapsody" contains a verse about someone dying painfully at a young age, though he never confirmed what the lyrics meant. Seventeen years after it was written, Freddie Mercury died from the AIDS virus, with his body aching, leaving everyone behind to face the truth.

Often, when a songwriter is asked how they wrote their song, their answer is, "I have no idea how I wrote this song," or "I didn't write this song; something else did," or "Something took over my body." This is not just limited to songs; this phenomenon can be found in the writing of movies or the painting of pictures—the artist has no idea how, why, when, where, and what they created. In the end, it's as if their work was created by a higher power.

Miracle ideas are waiting to be received, and all we have to do is quiet our minds to tap into one of them. Then it's up to us to act on one of these miracle ideas to bring it into creation. Thomas Edison believed that when he concentrated his thoughts, he was able to pick up on the ideas of others who thought similarly.[iii] Could it be that many of Edison's inventions were that of others who for whatever reason did not act?

While it's true that no one is exactly like you, there have been several recorded instances of two people, located in different parts of the world, who created the same—or similar—groundbreaking inventions at the same exact time. This has dumbfounded academics and scientists alike, but the rate of "simultaneous inventions" has increased over time.

These are inventions that happened at the exact same time on opposite sides of the world, as listed on qz.com:[iv]

1600s: Isaac Newton and Gottfried Leibniz both discovered calculus.

1770s: Carl Wilhelm Scheele and Joseph Priestley discovered oxygen.

1800s: Charles Darwin and Alfred Russel Wallace both describe natural selection.

1839: Louis Daguerre and Henry Fox Talbot invent the first photographic methods.

1869: Louis Ducos du Hauron and Charles Cros present the earliest workable methods of color photography on the same day.

1876: Alexander Graham Bell and Elisha Gray applied for a patent on the same exact day. Their invention: the telephone.

1950s: Jonas Salk and Albert Bruce Sabin invent the polio vaccine.

2015: Takaaki Kajita and Arthur B. McDonald are jointly awarded the Nobel prize for finding that neutrinos have mass.

Simultaneous inventions are due in part to the infinite field of "accessible knowledge" available to those who are able to hone in on it. It is possible that all the information we need for the human species to evolve peacefully and productively can be found in this invisible but accessible field of knowledge.

This sounds supernatural—how can invisible waves of information travel into the minds of humans? Well, this is exactly how our Wi-Fi works. Invisible radio waves are sent to other wireless devices that are tuned in to that specific frequency so that we can research information, watch videos, or play Temple Run if we like. So too can humans tap into the invisible frequencies of knowledge that are present in the quantum field surrounding all of us.

The imagination is much more powerful than we could imagine. Whenever we utilize our imagination, we literally converse with this invisible miracle force. The imagination can be quite unpredictable, and you never know when a life-changing idea can pop into your head if you allow it!

Manifesting Money

Everybody has heard a story like this: someone who needs $100K for a life-saving surgery happens to receive exactly $100K in some extraordinary way. I have heard these types of stories my entire life, but I always chalked it up to writer exaggeration. That is until it started happening to me.

Now, if it happens once or twice, I guess you could assume it's a coincidence, but what happens if it occurs so often that you know some unseen force is at play? I bet you could look back at your life and figure out a few times in which you needed a specific sum of money only to receive that exact amount. Looking back, I realized that this has occurred many times in my life—how in the world could I not have put two and two together sooner? Miracles happen in every aspect of our lives, especially when it comes to money!

While studying the Law of Attraction, I came across Rhonda Byrne's documentary "The Secret," which features interviews with people who experienced a miracle after applying this law in their lives. One of those interviewed was Jack Canfield, the uber-successful author of the Chicken Soup for the Soul series of books and education resources.

Jack Canfield said that his life changed forever, and he was able to manifest money beyond his wildest imagination when he met a gentleman by the name of W. Clement Stone. Mr. Stone was a businessman, philanthropist, and self-help author, who famously said, "Whatever the mind of man can conceive, it can achieve." He asked Canfield "to set a goal so big that, if he achieved it, it would blow his mind, and he'd know that it's only because of what he was taught that he would have achieved this goal."

While thinking about this challenge, Canfield pondered the idea of earning $100K for the year and living a $100K lifestyle. This was at a time when Canfield's earnings were only $8K per year. Although he had no strategy, and no possibility of earning $100K for the year, he said, "I'm gonna declare that I manifest $100K. I'm gonna believe it. I'm gonna act as if it's true and release it into the universe."

Mr. Stone's advice to Canfield was to "not only visualize the exact amount of money he'd desire" but, once he envisioned this amount, to write himself a check in the exact amount he desired. Canfield wrote a $100K check to himself and posted it above his bed, where he would see it morning and night. Shortly after writing the check, nothing major happened. One week went by, then two, then three, then an entire month. Then in the shower one day, a $100K idea popped into Canfield's head out of the blue. He had a book that was already written, and if he could sell 400K copies for the price of .25 each, he could earn $100K.

Jack Canfield didn't know how he was going to sell 400K copies, but then he saw a *National Enquirer* hanging in the magazine rack at the supermarket, which gave him the idea to market his book to readers. Six weeks later, he gave a talk to an audience of teachers, and at the end, a lady came up to him and said, "Jack, that was a great talk. I would like to interview you; let me give you my card." When Canfield looked at the card, it said *National Enquirer*—the same magazine that gave him the idea to market his book.[v]

After watching this documentary, I said to myself, "You know what, I will write myself a check for a specific dollar amount just like Jack Canfield did." On September 1, 2019, I wrote myself a check in the amount of $1M and stashed it away, hoping it would manifest by September 1, 2020. Even though I owned assets that were valued in the millions, I'd never even had close to that amount of money in my bank account, so it would pretty much be a miracle if it actually happened.

Even though I was convinced that there was some miracle force at work behind the scenes, the idea of me receiving $1M seemed like a long shot, if not impossible. I was a landlord with a number of profitable apartment buildings, but for many months I found myself taking losses. At the time, I probably had around $300K in cash spread out in a few different accounts, but I also had millions of dollars of debt. Most of the money I made was being shoveled out all over the place.

I was not totally convinced that I could manifest this amount of money, I didn't know exactly how I would be able to get $1M, but I was excited to give it a try. For the first few months after writing the check, nothing happened, and I didn't have any breakthrough ideas. I would soon forget about the check altogether.

In January of 2020, however, strange occurrence after strange occurrence began to happen. I really couldn't believe it. Whether it was stock trades that went in my favor, or money owed to me from years past, checks from all over the place started to come in. Additionally, debts that could have hurt me were wiped away or adjusted because of the COVID-19 pandemic, and for the first time in my life, after many years of struggle, I started to accumulate wealth.

I saw the Universe conspiring in my favor in all different ways, to a nearly unbelievable degree. My bank accounts went from $200k to $300k to $400k. I unloaded unprofitable investments, and my debt went from $5M to $4M to $3M. The less debt I had, the lighter I felt, while the more money I accumulated, the better I felt, and it was at this time that miracles not only became the norm, they became "the expected."

While this was all going on, a beautiful couple knocked on my door out of nowhere and wanted to buy my house in Staten Island. They loved my neighborhood and were infatuated with my house, and since they just sold their house in Brooklyn for an astronomical amount, they offered to buy my house for an equally astronomical amount. My house wasn't even listed, and I had no intention of moving. I mean, where would I even move to? But as miracle would have it, my wife and I found the house of our dreams in New Jersey, only twenty minutes from where we currently lived.

There were so many offers on the house in New Jersey, and it was a miracle that our offer was accepted. Thank goodness, because the thought of having to go back and tell the beautiful couple that we couldn't sell to them would have broken my heart more than the idea of not getting my dream home. Luckily, the Universe conspired in our favor. Both the couple that bought my house and the couple that sold us theirs were angels sent from above. It was as if this was some kind of prearranged divine agreement because I felt like I knew both couples on a soul level, if that makes sense. Whatever the case may be, this happened so effortlessly that my wife and I knew it was meant to be. It was a breath of fresh air to know that I wasn't the only one experiencing these miracles; my wife witnessed everything herself and even she began to question her reality!

There may be no more powerful way for the Universe to make Itself clear than when things fall into place so effortlessly and so miraculously that you know, beyond a shadow of a doubt, that you are at the right place at the right time, and this was meant to be.

While moving my stuff from my old house to my new house, I found the $1M check I wrote myself two years prior. My jaw dropped when I realized that the check was written on September 1, 2019. By September 1, 2021, I had well over a $1M in the bank and $0 in debt. The check that put me over $1M cleared on August 31, 2021, nearly two years to the day. What are the odds? If this didn't happen, I may not have written this book.

Even though it took me two years to reach my goal, instead of one, it happened: I manifested $1M. The fact that it happened on the same day and month in which I wrote the check in the first place left me with no doubt that the Universe was communicating with me. At this point, I was 100% convinced that I had cracked some type of success code by tapping into a force so powerful, so magical that miracles were now a daily occurrence.

Although money should not be the have-all-be-all, it does offer me freedom: freedom to be me. Freedom to learn. Freedom to grow. Freedom to do what I want to do when I want to do it. Freedom to write this book. Freedom to help other people succeed in this adventure we call life. And it wasn't just money that I attracted in my life; it was different people, thoughts, ideas, and inspirations, including much of the information you'll find in this book.

Nothing in my life changed until I tapped into Secret #1. Once I did, I didn't have to work harder or longer. I didn't have to take on any extra risk. I didn't have to go back to school or change careers. Nevertheless, if I could write a check for $1M and see it materialize, why not write a check for $5M? Which I already did!

In Conclusion

Life is a beautiful and magical experience. There are so many remarkable moments throughout the day, but sometimes we forget to notice because our focus is on our day-to-day frivolities. All we need to do is open our eyes, our hearts, and our minds to see the beauty in everything: the fluttering of a butterfly's wings, the marvelous cacophony of chirping birds, the song the leaves sing on a breezy spring day, the feeling of moist sand on the beach. Miracles are all around us!

For people who don't believe in miracles, please understand that life itself is a miracle! Remember, we live on a blue ball in the middle of an infinite Universe, and that blue ball is spinning at 1K miles per hour as it travels around a yellow-orange distant ball in the sky, which just so happens to be close enough to warm us but far enough not to melt us. If that's not enough, we have this protective covering known as our atmosphere, which surrounds Earth like a bubble and forms our beautiful blue sky, providing us with oxygen so we can breathe while protecting us from the sun's harmful rays. We have an invisible force known as gravity that allows us to move freely on the ground without having to worry about floating off into space. I could go on and on, but you get the point!

I'll say it again: miracles are the norm in life, not the exception. As soon as we realize this, miracles will show themselves in every way possible, whether it be receiving the exact amount of money at the exact time you needed it or meeting the love of your life because you made a right turn instead of a left.

Action Plan

Write yourself a check for a desired dollar amount. Hold that check in your hand. Look at that check and feel it as if the money is already yours. Continue to look at the dollar amount. Feel the dollar amount. Allow that feeling to sink into every cell of your body. See yourself with this money in the bank. Picture yourself looking at your bank account statement and seeing this exact amount. Give thanks to the Universe for providing you with this amount of money and know that you couldn't stop this amount of money from manifesting even if you tried.

Do you feel like a different person?

If you desire $10K, please write a check to yourself for $10K. If you desire $1M, please write a check for that amount to yourself. It is my personal experience that you should write a check for the maximum amount you desire. The amount that, if you earned it, would make you know it was solely because you tapped into Secret #1.

SECRET #2:
Circumstances in Life Don't Matter

"Waiting for circumstances in your life to change so you can feel good is like looking in a mirror waiting for your reflection to smile first." –Bashar

If someone offered you a billion dollars for your eyesight, would you give it up? Would you live life blind, unable to see, for a billion dollars? You would be rich. You could buy expensive art or whatever you wanted. You could get out of debt and travel the world. You could party with celebrities. All your so-called problems could disappear in a flash, except that you would be blind forever. Would you accept that offer?

Most, if not all, people would turn that offer down because when you cut through materialism, you realize that there are way more important things than stuff. So, if you wouldn't sell your eyesight for a billion dollars, you must already be a billionaire.

A challenge we have in our society is that our education system and television, radio, and media, in general, all work together to program us to believe we're lacking in something, be it money, education, attractiveness, or materialistic goods.

Schools may have initially been created with good intentions but later evolved into farm systems identifying talented and obedient corporate executives for people like Ford, Edison, and Carnegie. Unfortunately, school systems operate the same today as they did 100 years ago, punishing creative thinkers and rewarding the obedient.

How funny is it that television shows are also called programs? And doesn't the television "tell a vision"? The television "tells you" that to master life you must be rich or famous and "sells you" the idea that you're not rich unless you drive an expensive car, wear designer clothes, or live in a mansion. Unfortunately, this has many people going through life feeling poor, ugly, and basic because they don't look like a Victoria's Secret model, or they're not as rich as a Kardashian, or they don't live in a house that would be featured on *MTV Cribs*.

This type of programming is an important aspect of marketing and advertising, designed to get people to desire the things they don't have. It's used throughout society in the form of movies, television shows, commercials, and magazines to get people to think, act, work, and spend money the way the programmers want! Celebrities become major players in the game of "mind control over the masses"!

The reality is most things that truly matter in this world are free. We don't have to pay for oxygen; we don't have to pay for gravity; we don't have to pay for the physical body we come into this world with. We are born more abundant than the richest of men. We are born billionaires. And since you're already a billionaire, why not go through life with that assertion?

That doesn't mean you need to go out and purchase a Lamborghini or a Ferrari; that would be the fastest way to financial ruin. Trying to impress people with things is foolish. Especially when you're already a billionaire.

What feeling like a billionaire *does* mean is that while everyone else battles the feelings of day-to-day lack, you go on with the understanding and wisdom that you're more abundant than you could have ever imagined. **When we feel abundant, we attract more abundance!**

This is not theory; this is physics. The state of being we are in determines what we attract in our lives. **Everything we have, everything we do, everything we are, everything we will be in this life is determined by our state of being—which is the sum of our thoughts, our feelings, our beliefs, and our actions—especially our REACTIONS!**

Our *outer* world is a reflection of our *inner* world. **This is Secret #2: circumstances in life don't matter; it's our state of being that does. If we constantly focus on the emotions of pain, frustration, lack of abundance, and struggle, we amplify these energies and run the risk of attracting negative experiences that mirror our negative emotional state. On the other hand, if we focus and take action on the things that excite us, that make us healthier, that are more representative of our best and truest selves, we will attract more positive experiences that mirror our positive emotional state.**

Shatter Your Beliefs

Beliefs come in many forms. You may be consciously aware of your beliefs, or they can be deeply ingrained in the human psyche. For example, as a child, you may have overheard your parents talking about how money is the root of all evil and that people with money will never go to heaven. Now, you may not even remember your parents making this statement, but deeply ingrained in your mind is the idea that having money is bad. This may cause you to go through life deflecting money instead of attracting it.

The nonstop programming we face throughout our lives, so cleverly concealed in the movies we watch or the music we listen to, has a direct impact on the belief systems of the masses, allowing "the programmers" to steer society in whatever direction they see fit. As soon as you take control of your thoughts and beliefs and stop thinking like the herd, you start to break free from "the programming." **It's our beliefs that form our reality! Master your beliefs and you begin to master "the Matrix."**

If you believe life is unfair, you're right! If you believe life is fair, you're right! If you believe you'll fail, you're right! If you believe you'll succeed, you're right! If you believe money is the root of all evil, you're right! If you believe money can lead to ultimate freedom, you're right! You see, we are never wrong; the Universe will always support you in your beliefs. It won't argue with you! The Universe will even go out of its way to prove you're right by delivering you the exact outcome you *expected*!

We shatter limiting beliefs when we take action. It wasn't until I started building my business that I realized, "Wow, I didn't need nearly as much money as I thought I would to build my business." It wasn't until I started accumulating true wealth that I realized, "Wow, I didn't have to make nearly as much money as I thought I would to become financially independent." It wasn't until I started writing a book that I realized, "Wow, I didn't have to be a professional writer to write a book!"

With each shattered belief came a wealth of knowledge and wisdom. It wasn't before long that I realized the key that unlocks the door to the Matrix can be found in the debris and rubble of our newly shattered belief systems. Your beliefs can enslave you in the Matrix but by mastering them, by expanding your perceptions of reality, by expanding your idea of what's possible, you override lifelong programming, and you unlock the door to the Matrix. **You have the choice to exit the Matrix once you realize it was your beliefs that kept you there in the first place.**

As soon as I learned that it was my own beliefs that were holding me back all this time and that I had the power to change them, I began mastering life—not a second before!

I have studied the great thinkers and philosophers from the golden age of Greece through the age of the Enlightenment, all the way up to recent times, and I have not encountered a message as important as Bashar's for the overall advancement of humanity. This book would not be possible without the help and insight of this great being. What an honor it has been to work with him and his team to make this book a reality. Below is Bashar's magnificent description of how to identify and change a belief that is deeply ingrained in our psyche.

Bashar—How to Change a Core Belief

Your beliefs are the blueprint of your physical experience. You can't live in a house until it's built, and you don't begin building until you have the blueprint first. That's your foundation! Everything is built on belief, so anytime your thoughts, feelings, and behavior seem to be out of alignment with what you prefer, you can always trace them back to the belief that generated them because feelings don't just come from nowhere. You can't actually experience an emotion unless you have a definition first; if you don't know the definition of something, you have absolutely no idea how to feel about it.

Let's take the word "brontide." What feeling do you get from the word itself? Because you do not know the definition, you do not get a feeling from the word. It's only until you learn that brontide can be explained as being a low, muffled sound similar to distant thunder, that you elicit any feeling from the word.

You are taught definitions when you are growing up; you absorb them through body language, through telepathy, from your parents, your society, from all around you. The thing about it is it happens so unconsciously that you don't even realize until later that you've been fed a library of definitions that you're then having feelings, thoughts, and behaviors about as a response to those definitions. But if you weren't fed those definitions, you wouldn't be having any thoughts about it at all.

For example, in your society, the definition of "paying bills" is quite negative. However, if you look at it from another perspective, with each paid bill, a business can add jobs, individuals can put food on the table, and your payment can benefit society in ways you never realized. We are not saying to run up debts to prove this theory correct. All we're saying is that by changing your definition of "paying bills," you change the feeling you get out of it. So, from now on, when you pay a bill—think of it as a donation that will go to benefit humanity, instead of "the dreaded bill payment."

If you want to feel more empowered, think of yourself as the boss of your own company, and with every check you write in the form of a bill, envision yourself paying the salary of one of your employees instead of paying a greedy company out to get you. These companies DO work for you! You are their employer! Without you, they don't exist! You're not only their boss, but you're also their savior! So, act like it!

Master Your State of Being, Master Your World

Your thoughts, your emotions, your words, your actions, and your conscious and unconscious beliefs all work together to create your state of being. You'll know what state of being you're in by the way you react to circumstances that pop up in your life. True life masters react positively or neutrally to any circumstances, no matter how bad they may seem on the surface. How do you react when something in life doesn't seem to go your way?

Remaining in a low energetic and depressed state of being is like "watching" an awful television show because the remote is too far away. Do you continue to watch the terrible show, or do you stand up, walk across the room, grab the remote, and change the channel yourself? Do you continue to allow the same "non-preferable" reality in your life to play out, or do you change it?

First, you must desire change. Then you must become determined to change. Then you must act on that desire and determination by taking one step in the direction of the person you desire to be because as soon as you do, that is when the tide will turn. Just like a single snowflake causing an avalanche, one step in the direction of your best self is all that may take to change your focus, change your energy, change your emotions, change your beliefs, and eventually change your "television station" to something more compatible with the life of your dreams.

Just fifteen minutes of focused intent on whatever it is you desire to do or whoever it is you desire to be is all you may need to get the ball rolling. Spend fifteen minutes making a to-do list, an idea list, a goal list, or an intention list; whatever you want to call it. Maybe you can spend fifteen minutes creating an outline for the book you always wanted to write. Maybe you can spend fifteen minutes exercising, meditating, or learning a new skill. You don't even need to get up off the couch; you can spend fifteen minutes of your focused intention visualizing the perfect life for yourself. Visualizing and dreaming and planning are great to start, don't get me wrong, but in the long run, you just can't dream; you must take physical action. Repeat this process day after day and be open to the idea of being guided by miracles, synchronicities, inspirations, and continuous feelings of excitement.

Warning: while following your excitement, you may lose track of time and that's quite all right! So don't be surprised if you plan to spend fifteen minutes on something that interests you and suddenly three hours go by in a flash! "Time flies when you're having fun" isn't just a catchphrase. It's the most ancient of wisdom!

When you have certain thoughts dancing around in your mind, whether it be a lack of abundance or lack of self-worth, to dismantle it you may have to trace that thought back to its source. You may find out that your lack of self-worth was handed down to you by parents, schoolmates, exes, or wicked stepmothers who made you feel that way because by doing so, it crushed your confidence, causing you to dim your light, giving these people momentary satisfaction of superiority over you. What you may not know is the judgment heaped on you by others throughout your life was, and probably still is, the same thing these individuals judge about themselves. People often project their insecurities onto others. For example, those who fear becoming overweight may judge others based on their weight. Those who fear being poor will judge others based on their financial status. Once you realize that everyone's opinion of you is based on their insecurities, you can go on and laugh when someone says something bad about you because you now know that's exactly what they fear and exactly what they judge about themselves. Forget others' opinions of you; what do you believe is true about yourself?

> *Once a person wraps their mind around the understanding that they never had to buy into others' beliefs, and as soon as this is realized, they break free from that programming. Imagine how powerful and indestructible they are from that point forward. –Bashar*

Remember, when you start reacting differently to circumstances and situations that previously left you feeling angry, frustrated, or victimized, that's how you'll know you are beginning to master your state of being.

Expand Your Perception of Abundance

By expanding your definition and perception of abundance you may just realize that you are way more abundant than previously thought, and going forward you don't have to suffer the feelings of day-to-day lack so many of us experience. Let me prove your abundance to you.

Bashar's philosophy regarding abundance was truly life-changing for me!

Bashar on Abundance:

Abundance is something that offers you the ability to do what you need to do when you need to do it. That's the true definition of abundance. There are many forms of abundance, but we are going to discuss the five major forms that you experience in your reality so that you can begin to understand that abundance is not limited to what you were taught to believe about wealth and empowerment. Below, we will speak about the five forms of abundance most common in your world so that you can open up to all the various forms of abundance and allow them to support you and serve you in a more synchronistic way in your life.

#1. Money

First and foremost, let us begin with the most common form of abundance called money. There is a great deal of focus on this particular form of abundance in our society. Now, there is nothing wrong with the idea whatsoever. Money is simply a way of saying that you have decided and agreed, in a form of consensus reality, that there should be some article, some artifact that symbolizes the power of exchange, whether it be paper or metal coins.

Money is the form of abundance that you are most familiar with, but many of you focus on this particular form of expression way more than any other form, even to the point where you close the door to the other types of abundance that can appear in your life.

For many of you, money is really the type of abundance that is most powerful and one that can allow you to do what you need to do when you need to do it, which, after all, is the definition of abundance itself. But it's not the only one; there are four other major forms of abundance you can experience on your planet and can experience more often if you allow it.

#2. Trade or Barter

The second one is simply the idea of trade. If you have something someone else wants, be it an object or a skill, you can trade for it because it allows you to do what you need to do in life when you need to do it! So, trading or bartering is an old form of abundance that predates the idea of money, but money has, for the most part, replaced it in your world.

#3. Receiving or Giving a Gift

The third form is simply to be given a gift. Gifts are a form of abundance when they are given to support someone. Gifts are given to you, and they can help you do what you need to do in life to survive. Gifts are absolutely a valid form of abundance, and you never know when someone might come along and give you something you don't necessarily need to pay for or need to trade anything for, other than the gratitude that you express in receiving a gift, which is also a form of exchange.

*Sometimes individuals in your society, when it comes to the idea of giving or receiving gifts, are a little reluctant to receive them. Some give and give and give but are reluctant to receive because they think that there must be something wrong with that. There is absolutely nothing wrong with it, and if you look at it from another point of view, **the idea of allowing someone to give to you is a form of giving to them because they get as much joy from giving as you get from receiving.** So, be willing to receive when it happens because receiving is also a form of giving, as it allows them to experience a similar feeling.*

#4. Synchronicity

The next form of abundance is synchronicity itself. When you are moving through life and you come upon the exact information you need to hear, the exact object you needed at the time, or you meet the exact person you needed to meet at that exact moment you needed to meet them to help you continue on your path—that is synchronicity.

Synchronicity can supply you with an understanding, a bit of information, or a bit of inspiration, which can assist you on your journey so you can continue to keep moving on your path of least resistance, on your path of highest passion. Synchronicity is a form of abundance, as it simply goes back to the definition of giving you the ability to do what you need to do when you need to do it.

#5. Imagination, Inspiration, and Creative Expression

The fifth form of abundance is imagination, inspiration, and creative expression. The idea is that when you allow your imagination, which is a conduit of communication between yourself and your higher mind, to be open in a balanced way, imagination and inspiration can provide you with a new idea, a new path, and new information that you can use to perhaps change the course of your life or do something you didn't think of doing before but that may be more representative of your true path. **Creative expression is a form of abundance and vital for an overall feeling of fulfillment and happiness.**

Putting It All Together

So, the idea of money, the idea of trade, the idea of gift-giving, the idea of synchronicity, and the idea of your creative expression make up the five major forms of abundance that can exist in your reality. Most people on your planet close the doors to all other forms of abundance except money. They may think that the other four types of abundance don't get you what you need, but very often these other forms of abundance can be the path of least resistance in your life and can give you what you need and can support you even more quickly sometimes than the idea of money.

This is fundamentally how it works: when you follow your passion, the five forms of abundance may show up in all different combinations to support you. For example, sometimes you may experience the first and second forms of abundance or the third or fourth or any other combination of forms; it doesn't have to come in just one way or in just one form. Very often it comes more efficiently if you will be open to allowing all the forms to come in when and how they need to, to work together to create the support that you need. So, sometimes you may find yourself getting a "little bit of money" and then synchronicity will appear, or a gift will be given to you, or you will be inspired by something that will provide you more abundance, or perhaps you can trade something that will add to your ability to live abundantly.

The idea is to allow the proportions and the ratios to form the one hundred percent version of abundance that you need, but that one hundred percent may be made of a little more of this and a little more of that. Let it come in that way because that is usually representative of the easiest way, the path of least resistance for you, and when you are open to all the forms of abundance, things happen in a much more accelerated way.

Expand Your Perceptions of Reality

Begin to question everything you think, know, or believe to be true in this world. Inaccurate thinking, erroneous beliefs, insistence on being right, hubris, and ego all work together to enslave you and entrap you in a world of self-limitation. It's okay to be wrong. It's okay not to know something. It's okay to ask for advice.

Don't go around correcting everyone because a person's truths are theirs; your truths are yours. Forcing your beliefs on someone is futile. Wisdom lies in knowing that everyone is on their path, and quite possibly part of their journey is for them to make mistakes, to learn from them, and to grow from them without outside interference from you. Don't argue or offer your unwanted advice. Instead, lead by example.

Thinking you know everything is like being tuned to one radio station, listening and believing everything the radio station says because that's the only station you believe exists. If you're open to the idea that there are many different radio stations playing at the same time, you may just tap into the radio station—that will attract knowledge, opportunity, wisdom, creativity, and wonderful ideas that can support you on your greatest path. Stop talking and begin to listen because you never know when someone may say something that causes a light bulb to go off in your head, sparking a life-changing thought or idea.

Beliefs can encourage us, or they can enslave us. If you think you know everything, you will be trapped in your own little bubble, never to get out until you open to the ideas and perspectives of others.

Throughout my life, I've been around some of the most successful people in the world, and I've also been around some who were rather unsuccessful. It's the unsuccessful people who believe they know everything. It's the unsuccessful people who only answer questions and never ask them. It's the unsuccessful person who will correct you and tell you that you are wrong or that your ideas are crazy.

Remember, what a person believes to be true is true for them. Beliefs are a person's interpretation of reality. It's like looking at an art painting: two people may have different interpretations of the same painting, but neither is right nor wrong. What one sees in the painting is based on their knowledge of art, current emotions, life experiences, beliefs, and senses.

It's my experience that those who are wise tend to be flexible with their beliefs, knowing that as they evolve so, too, can their outlook on life. In contrast, someone who is inflexible and rigid in their beliefs may never change, and this can enslave them in an unpreferable reality.

Remember what we have said: to master your reality, you need to master your understanding of belief systems and how they operate to empower you or limit you.

We Manifest What We Believe We Can

Almost everyone has heard the story of the four-minute mile. I'll explain. Legend has it that experts throughout history have said that it was impossible to run a mile in under four minutes. For thousands of years, the feat was never accomplished. That was until May 6, 1954, when Roger Bannister ran a mile in 3:59.4. A year after Roger did it, another person accomplished the feat, then a few more, until now, for many strong runners, it's almost routine to run a four-minute mile. What's interesting is that "as part of his training, [Roger Bannister] relentlessly visualized the achievement to create a sense of certainty in his mind and body."[vi]

Roger Bannister's story is not an isolated event. Growing up, I experienced firsthand the power of belief.

A friend of mine was one of the best high school baseball players in the country for his age. When he graduated, he was immediately drafted by the Atlanta Braves, and in two short years, at the age of twenty, he was pitching alongside a rotation that featured Hall-of-Famers Greg Maddux, Tom Glavine, and John Smoltz. Jason Marquis not only became a major league all-star and World Series pitcher, but he was also consistently one of the best hitters and fielders throughout his long career.

In the last twenty years since Jason became a major league star, there have been more players from Staten Island drafted by a major league team than in the previous hundred years combined. When a person accomplishes the impossible, oftentimes they act as a guide and a beacon of hope for others to potentially follow in their footsteps.

Some people may avoid living their best lives or becoming their best selves just because they're comfortable. They will deflect success because success equals change, and change leads them into the unknown. For many, including myself, the unknown was scary; it was unpredictable, but it was in the unknown that I discovered a better version of myself. It was in the unknown where I accomplished what I previously thought was impossible. I always thought I'd encounter some type of evil while venturing on the unknown path; however, the only thing I found on this path was a better, more experienced version of myself. From my perspective, the devil dwells far away from the "unknown" in a place we call the "comfort zone." The unknown is where we'll find our greatest selves!

Do not fear the unknown. Holding on to this negative belief is a choice. Transform your negative beliefs. Exorcise your limitations. Begin to believe that you can achieve the impossible. Remember, what you believe to be true about life and about yourself can either propel you to new heights or keep you trapped in a prison of doubt, worry, and fear!

You are the writer, the director, the star actor, and the main critic of your own reality! What you focus your attention on, what you believe to be possible, what you act on, and the story you tell others about yourself constructs your reality!

How do you define your reality? Is it a reality of struggle, pain, and suffering, or a wonderful, exciting adventure? You get to choose. Choose wisely, because whatever you choose, you'll experience!

Bashar on the idea of beliefs and manifestation:

*Any degree of difficulty, pain, and suffering you have ever experienced is not because there is actually inherent difficulty built into life and creation. All that pain comes from the perspective that is created by the belief systems within our unconscious mind. **What you manifest in your life is based on what you believe is possible for you.** The question is, what do you believe is possible?*

If you believe you will not be able to get a specific job because you think people don't like you or that they will judge you, then chances are your body language, your verbiage, your actions, and your attitude will most likely make that belief a reality. Maybe during the interview your shoulders slump, you slouch in your chair, you don't look people in the eyes, you don't smile— all in all, you don't exude confidence in yourself.

It's the same type of scenario with relationships. Let's say you really like someone, and you want to make a good impression, but you're scared because you believe that this person may not like you, especially since you've not had success recently in relationships. How this belief plays out is similar: during your date, your mind goes through the file system of beliefs in your head while the other person is talking. You think, "The last few relationships of mine were complete failures; maybe it's me. Am I not attractive? Do I not have a good personality?" You are having a discussion with yourself instead of having a carefree discussion with the person you are speaking to. This may cause you to forget what the other person is even talking about, creating an uncomfortable scenario in which the original speaker begins to question the natural flow of the relationship.

Have confidence; do not fear rejection! If other people reject you, so what? They have nothing to do with your dream, your soul's path, your journey, or your destination; so, why do you care? Why are you accepting their opinion of you?

In Conclusion

All the difficulty, pain, and suffering on our planet occur from someone attempting to manipulate their reflection in the mirror instead of changing themselves. We control our reflection. The mirror cannot change the reflection, only you can. So, stop waiting for some outside circumstance to change your inner self, because when you change on the inside, the reflection in the mirror has no choice but to change.

Think of your thoughts and emotions as a compass, and wherever it points, you go. Your compass can bring you to a Caribbean Island or slam you into an iceberg! Take control of your compass and have it work for you so it can point you in a direction more representative of your greatest self. Remember, whatever we believe to be true generates the emotions we feel, and our emotions produce the thoughts we think, our recurring thoughts influence our actions, and our actions create our future experiences. That's how powerful our state of being is!

Last but not least, stop reacting negatively to your circumstances; stop reacting at all. Stay neutral. As Bashar says, "Nothing in life has built-in meaning; therefore, it's up to us to give it meaning. The meaning we give it is the effect we get out of it. This goes for relationships, behaviors, beliefs, fears, occurrences, perspectives, experiences, and life in general. Circumstances in life don't matter; our reaction to them and our state of being does. So, react positively to everything that occurs in your life, and you will no longer suffer the pain and agony felt when something did not "go your way.""

Action Plan

The challenges and circumstances that arise throughout life present a wonderful opportunity for us to discover our power within. So great is this inner force that once it's activated, it can be called upon at will to help you overcome any challenge or circumstance you may face in the future. The greater the challenge or circumstance you overcome, the more powerful this inner force becomes. The best part is that the ability to call upon this inner force is a superpower, and whoever can master this ability can master their reality!

Below is an exercise intended to help you activate this inner power so you can become the person you are truly meant to be. The "powerful you." The "great you." The "you" who you will become. The "you" who you truly are!

Step 1: To activate your inner power, all you need to do is think of a time in your life when you felt empowered and recreate that same feeling in your mind and body. Yes, it's as simple as that. Just by thinking about an experience from your past, and by making an intention to recreate that feeling, we can activate this inner force and call upon it whenever we so choose.

If you're having trouble recreating a feeling of empowerment from past experiences, then just imagine the greatest version of yourself in the future. What does that "empowered you" look like? How does that "empowered you" talk? How does that "empowered you" walk? How did that "empowered you" become empowered in the first place?

Step 2: Now think of the greatest victory you could imagine and recreate *that* scintillating feeling of empowerment and excitement and feel it throughout the mind and body all at once. Truly sensationalize this feeling, as if every cell in your body feels that victory as if it was the greatest victory of your life.

By doing this, you have now unlocked a technique that is used by some of the greatest people throughout history and knowing that you have the power to empower yourself is all the power you need to master this reality! That is the victory of all victories if you ask me!

Let's spend one minute truly mastering this technique.

Step 3: Continue to visualize the "greatest you" winning the "greatest victory," as if it was the greatest feeling possible. Concentrate that feeling into a ball and see that energy ball float six inches above the top of your head. Next, feel the ball move down to the middle of the eyebrow. Envision the ball of energy touching the middle of the brow and feel that euphoric warmth. Then picture this empowering and euphoric ball of energy traveling down to your throat, warming each area it encounters. Continue to feel that empowering euphoria and envision this energy traveling down onto the middle of your chest, then the top of your stomach, then to the belly button, feeling that ball of energy stop at each location for a few seconds and finally stopping at the ankles. Then feel this energy go down your arms and your legs. Then for five seconds, flex every muscle you can in both your arms and your legs at the same time, glutes included. While you're clenching these muscles for five seconds, continue to flood the brain with nonstop feelings of well-being. Then relax for ten seconds. After the ten-second relaxation period is up, flex the muscles again and get excited for another five seconds! Allow your entire body to vibrate with the euphoric feelings of power, excitement, and joy while flexing your muscles for five seconds, and then relax the entire body, as if you are floating on a cloud, weightless, for ten seconds. Repeat this exercise four times for a total of sixty seconds.

If you want to do it longer, go ahead. This exercise will reset your body's magnetic frequency; it will activate both hemispheres of the brain at once. I believe, quite often, a person's level of greatness can be attributed to their ability to activate both the right hemisphere and the left hemisphere of the brain simultaneously, making them superhuman, both physically and mentally. It's how people break bricks, lift cars, or do things physically that boggle the mind. Begin to activate this ability within yourself by repeating this activity a few times a day.

Step 4: Now, relax the jaw, then relax the entire body. Then take a deep breath through the nose for a count of four seconds.

Hold your breath for a count of eight seconds. Exhale through the mouth for a count of twelve seconds and continue to feel all the tension and stress leave your body.

Step 5: Again, continue to relax the jaw and the entire body. Then take a deep breath through the nose for a count of four seconds. Hold your breath for a count of eight seconds. Exhale through the mouth for a count of twelve seconds and continue to feel all the tension and stress leave your body.

Just a Thought

Greatness has more to do with mastering the mind than it does with having talent or being born with a high IQ. It's why the C student becomes the boss of the A student. It's why a less physically gifted athlete can dominate over opponents who are bigger, faster, and stronger. He who masters his mind masters his world!

If feelings of doubt, guilt, fear, or any other negative emotion arise in your life, at any time, give thanks to those emotions because without them, the feeling of empowerment wouldn't feel as empowering. Stop worrying! Stop holding yourself back! Stop being who you are not! Stop now!

Start creating! Start doing what you love! Start small! Start now!

SECRET #3:
The Universe Conspires in Our Favor

It may seem as if everything in life is falling apart,
when in reality, it's all falling into place.

Shortly after I began investing in real estate, I got a call from my property manager at 3:00 a.m., telling me that my investment was on fire. I didn't know how bad it was, but I had about thirty missed calls and many more texts. I couldn't believe it. I had to drive to the property to see it myself.

When I was about four miles from the building, I could see fire engines and police cars flying by me. I said, "Please don't let that be my property." About a quarter mile from the apartment building, I saw every street blocked off. I had never seen this before in my life.

Sure enough, eighty-seven firemen were tasked with putting out the fire to my apartment building. I had moved heaven and earth to buy what I believed was a decent investment opportunity. I had spent a considerable amount of time and money fixing it up. But now all I could picture were my tenants burning in a fire, many of whom had beautiful young children. I was shaking and sure my life was over.

Luckily, not one person was hurt in the fire, and I thank the Lord that that was the case. I knew the situation was bad, but at least I didn't have to live with the guilt of one of my tenants perishing in a fire. What little money I had in my bank account at this time was given to the tenants to relocate.

The fire was extinguished, the tenants were relocated, and now the damage had to be assessed. It's not like the bank calls you and tells you that you don't have to pay the loan after a house burns; they want their money on the first of the month regardless.

I wondered if I had the stomach for this type of investing. This property, which I had purchased a year prior, had been wiped away overnight. I didn't have the money to rebuild the house, I owed money on credit cards, I owed money in loans, basically I owed money everywhere, and I was no longer getting rent on this building. I asked a seasoned investor if this had ever happened to him, and after knocking on wood, he said emphatically, "No, NEVER EVER HAS ANYTHING LIKE THIS HAPPENED TO ME!"

My goodness, what in the world was I to do at this point? Where to begin? What good could come out of this? The fire was said to have been caused by a lightning strike. What were the odds? Was this a sign from God? I almost wished the lightning had struck me instead.

At this point in time, I certainly did not believe the Universe was conspiring in my favor, so I was quite emotional. However, I *was* a believer in the idea that "all things happen for a reason," which gave me hope for the time being, even though I was unsure what the reason was.

When I finally regrouped emotionally, I began to figure out the next steps to take. I called the insurance company to make sure that I had the correct protection on the building, and then I crossed my fingers and prayed to God I would receive enough money to at least pay back the loan. To add insult to injury, two weeks before this fire was Hurricane Sandy, which damaged many homes along the East Coast USA, and insurance companies were backlogged for months and months. My entire life relied on the decision of my insurance company to give me the money to rebuild the property.

With my entire life on the line, the insurance adjuster called me with bad news. He told me that he was *only* able to get me just enough money to rebuild the property, but nothing more. Little did he know that I was celebrating and jumping for joy because there was a possibility I would receive nothing. At least now I'd be able to rebuild the property *and* pay off some of my debts. And that's exactly what I did. It wasn't pretty, since this was the first investment property I built from the ground up, and there were many ups and downs regarding the building process, but I was able to complete the construction and re-rent the property.

This scenario was horrible, and I wish this on no one, but I learned how to build, which would come in handy later in my life. I also now had a property that was basically brand-new, made more money, and would cost less in maintenance for the foreseeable future. It became one of my best investments.

This is one example in which the Universe seems to conspire in our favor, especially if we have a neutral or positive attitude. Looking back at my life, I noticed that every failure of mine—and there were many, whether it be an involuntary career change or a financial catastrophe—was nothing more than road signs directing me, guiding me, sometimes pushing, pulling, or even twisting me into the best version of myself.

With the right attitude, every step, every experience, every miscalculation, and every failure can strengthen your resolve to a point where you become this new unbreakable version of yourself. "Whatever doesn't kill you makes you stronger" is not just a catchphrase, it's the most ancient of wisdom!

> ## Bashar's Rubber Band Analogy:
>
> When you are at a low, when everything around you seems to be falling apart, like a rubber band, you pull it back farther and farther into the darkness so that when you finally let go, you will fly that much faster and that much stronger and that much farther into the light!

Secret #3 is that the Universe is and has always been conspiring in our favor.

As soon as I realized this secret, and for the first time in my life, the Universe rapidly began to conspire for me instead of against me. In learning this secret my life changed overnight, and no longer did I view a negative experience as bad.

If you want to get the Universe on your side, you need to first realize that **the Universe *is* and *has* always been on your side!** Even if an experience does not seem pleasant at the time, you need to understand that it was the very experience you needed to have in your life to help you learn, grow, and become a better version of yourself.

Becoming Our Best Selves

I could probably write a novel about one of the best salesmen and successful businessmen in New York City, Dominick Russo. Dominick is a first-generation Italian American who would tell you that his mother and father emigrated from Calabria, Italy "with their luggage only, and just enough money to afford a plane ticket to get here." That didn't stop him from being a success. Dominick is now the President and owner of an enormously successful insurance and investment firm, and many of the financial lessons I learned came from the trials and tribulations of his life.

When I was in college around 1998, the stock market was booming. Dominick was a stockbroker and a close friend of mine, and I interned with him during the summer months and in between college semesters. During this time, I witnessed monthly checks for hundreds of thousands of dollars pile up in his bank account.

Dominick was around the age of twenty-five, earning close to seven figures a year. I didn't have a dollar to my name, but Dominick was rich, and he spent money like it would never run out. He drove the best cars and spent thousands every time we went out; I remember watching him lose $15K in Atlantic City without a care in the world. I rode on the back of his motorcycle as he was driving 100 miles per hour, and a few times, we almost went down. We lived a very fast life, and we were both lucky to be alive.

I couldn't wait to join Dominick and his firm as soon as I graduated college, but sadly in 2001, the stock market went south. Nearly every investment collapsed overnight. Dominick would lose most of his fortune along with his clients. Lawsuits followed, and it was as if Dominick was staring down a long dark hallway that would never end. Before he lost his money, he was prepared to purchase a beautiful property for pennies on the dollar, but his chances of buying that lot crashed with the stock market.

Dominick could have quit, he could have thrown in the towel, but that wasn't him. Dominick fast life slowed to a halt, he found a beautiful wife, and he traded in an S600 Mercedes Benz for a minivan, literally. This transformation was amazing because I could almost guarantee that God saved Dominick's life—and maybe mine, for that matter.

I watched Dominick reinvent himself like never before. He started his own firm, began selling different types of insurance products, and twelve years later, he wound up earning more money than he did in the late '90s. Not only did he reinvent himself, but he built a much more stable business that revolved around earning set commissions, known as residuals, which grew his monthly income to astronomical numbers. Many brokers who Dominick worked with were slow to reinvent themselves and were struggling, but he was a self-made millionaire for the second time. He went from riches to rags, back to riches, and with that, he built a massive business that thrives to this day.

Dominick frequently says that the best thing that ever happened to him was losing all his money, because not only did it add about twenty years to his life, but it also allowed him to build a more lucrative and stable business for the future. Often, our most troubling experiences are nothing more than our greatest blessings, because they teach us valuable lessons so that we can be the best person we can possibly be, financially, physically, emotionally, and spiritually!

There are no accidents; the Universe seems to be always conspiring in our favor. Once we realize the UNIVERSE is always serving our best interest, we can lighten up on ourselves because no longer do we have to live with anxiety and fear of a vengeful force surreptitiously making our life hell.

Imagine going through life knowing that, with the right attitude, even the most negative experience can be used to serve us in a beneficial way? What could we then accomplish? Would there be any limit to our potential? Think back in your life: can you think of a time in which something you thought was a nightmare actually turned out to be a blessing?

Avoiding Disaster

The Universe conspires in our favor, and in many circumstances, it acts as a guardian angel. For example, there are stories of people who uncharacteristically missed their flight, only to find out later that the plane they so fortunately missed had crashed. Or someone had car trouble on the morning of 9/11, only to hear on the radio that their office was hit by a plane and everyone at work that day perished in the disaster.

I'll never forget the time in 2002, coming home from a job interview in Manhattan when I walked into a Starbucks and there were only a few people ahead of me, but for some reason, the baristas were taking a very long time. I remember pondering whether I should hurry up and catch the boat home or wait in the Starbucks line. I gave it a few more minutes, but the line didn't budge, so I ran out to catch the boat home from Manhattan to Staten Island cursing the barista's the entire way. I rushed to the terminal and literally was the last person to get on the boat. The deckhand was kind enough to unlock the chain to let me on.

About twenty minutes after I got off the boat in Staten Island, I started to get phone calls from people asking me if I was okay, but I couldn't understand why. I was told that the captain of the ferry after mine had a medical episode, and the ferry crashed into the pier, killing a number of passengers who were on board.

I couldn't believe it. I certainly didn't have a good feeling after that; actually, I had some anxiety for a while because I was the last person on the earlier boat.

Later on, in my spiritual journey, I would learn that we should never doubt the Universe. If something happens to us that causes us to be late, take it as a sign that the Universe is protecting us from something that could be far worse. With that being said, thank goodness there was a line that didn't move at all in Starbucks, because if I'd waited the extra few minutes, who knows what could have happened to me? Thank goodness the workers were slow that day.

Now, I know what some of you may be thinking: what about the people on the boat who were killed? If the Universe is always on our side, then why do some of us die tragically? The reason I say this is because these were the exact questions I had for Bashar.

Bashar's explanation of death changed my life, and I think it bears repeating because many people fear death, and the idea of dying can be psychologically crippling throughout a person's life.

Bashar's explanation of death:

You will leave Earth when you're ready to leave. You will not leave one second before you're ready, but you will not leave one second later than you're ready. Do you understand? You already chose the timing of your death, and because you chose the timing, you will know that whatever it is, and whenever it is, it will be perfect according to what you chose. So, you don't have to think about it, and you don't have to worry about it. If you were ready to leave, you would have gone, and if you were done with this life, you would have left. It's that simple. Something would have happened to cause you to die, and since you didn't die, you're not done. It's that simple. Will you breathe easier now?

There have been times when people got into a car accident only to find out they were hit by their future spouse, and they never would have met them had it not been for the car accident. I know one person who, after spending weeks and months in a hospital, learned so much about anatomy and physiology that he later became a doctor.

Bashar on the idea of car accidents:

Car accident—how exciting! What did you get out of the experience you otherwise wouldn't have learned if you hadn't got into an accident? The lesson may take some time to come to light, but if you choose to stay positive or neutral, it'll be much easier to figure out why you may have generated that experience for yourself. Maybe the reason has something to do with your life's purpose!

Even a broken heart can be a blessing in disguise. Like Bashar says, "Sometimes relationships fail because our significant other is nothing more than a symbol of our thoughts, emotions, and beliefs regarding ourselves at that current moment. However, if a relationship does not 'work out' or 'come to fruition,' but you know that you learned a lot from it, just by being in that positive state, you can attract the exact person you need in your life at the perfect time." When you become the best you, don't be surprised if you attract the best person for that version of you.

In Conclusion

The ring manager called out, "John, are you ready to go?" And just like that, the biggest UFC match of his life was ready to begin. John was a few wins away from one of the very first UFC titles ever, but his current opponent was a 6'4" inch monster who needed 2 scales to weigh in.

No one would be crazy enough to fight Gary "Big Daddy" Goodridge, a UFC legend before UFC was well known, when there were barely any weight classes, when there were barely any rules. But here he was on this day, John Campetella, a 5'10" fighter.

John was built like a bull and quite possibly just as intimidating as Goodridge, but he was not well known at this time. This was his chance to prove himself to the world by becoming a UFC champion, a UFC legend, a UFC GOD.

Most people would run away or fake an injury when seeing the size of his opponent, but John wasn't scared. He didn't fight because he wanted to win; he fought because he wanted to kill. It was killer vs. killer.

The crowd cheered, jeered, hollered, and cursed as John walked down the aisle of the arena before stepping into "THE OCTAGON," which was nothing more than an 8-sided chain-link fence, 6 feet high and 30 feet across, more suitable for a prison yard than a professional fight. The cage was meant to keep fighters in the ring, denying them their biological flight response, leaving only the option to stand and fight!

Both fighters met in the middle of the ring for some quick instructions from the ref, and ding, ding, ding, the bell rang. John came out firing shots at Goodridge, but Goodridge was so tall that John had to leap in the air to punch his head—and that's just what he did. One shot to the head, one shot to the body, another shot to the head, and within the first moments of the fight, Gary Goodridge looked lost. Goodridge didn't block the shots, didn't try to throw a punch; he turned around as if he was ready to climb out of the steel cage.

John was confused; the ref was confused; everyone in the arena was confused. The fans didn't want a winner—they wanted blood. What was going on? Gary Goodridge, the person the UFC hyped up to win this tournament, the person UFC needed to win the tournament, looked as if he was ready to quit.

After the shots rang out on the head of Goodridge, John grabbed his opponent and ripped him down to the floor. Both fighters came crashing down, but Gary Goodridge was able to hold on to the steel cage and balance himself.

From a business standpoint, no one knew John Campetella at this time, he was not promoted, so a Campetella victory could potentially hurt the pockets of the UFC owners. Luckily for the UFC, Goodridge was able to throw one punch at John while John was trying to regain his footing. The ref then stopped the fight prematurely at 1.28 seconds, in favor of Gary Goodrich.

Campetella, the crowd, and everyone who watched the fight were confused. In moments, John's chance at a UFC title was over. His fighting career was seemingly over. John was winning the fight and most likely would have won the fight had it not been called early, but that's not how it unfolded.

As John walked out of the ring cursing the refs, cursing Goodridge and all who stepped in his path, the same manager who had led him out to the ring said, "Listen, kid, I'm sorry. The league didn't get a chance to build you up yet. It's not your time right now."

However, as John would learn, the Universe is and has always been conspiring in our favor. Although he did not win that fight, and his professional fighting career ended, he would eventually take a different route to success. Shortly after UFC, John went on to NYU, where he would excel academically and later become a college professor. In addition to teaching, John would go on to own and operate numerous successful businesses. And now in his 50s, he works out all the time, is in the same shape he was in 30 years ago, and has more money than he knows what to do with.

What would have happened if John Campetella had won that match? How would his life have turned out had he become UFC champion of the world? It's a question he has asked himself often. I know because I happen to have a front-row seat to his mind since John is a good friend and business partner.

If John had continued fighting in the UFC, he could have been another washed-up fighter with injuries. He could have lost everything like many fighters do after years in the ring. Instead, he became a total success.

I don't think there's any debate, John lucked out losing that fight. Whether it's being fired from a job or causing a breakup for our own good, the Universe ingeniously orchestrates the best possible long-term scenario for every one of us. So just relax. Let go.

Trust in the timing of everything. If you're late for work, or if you miss a flight, or if you are stuck in traffic, take it as a sign that the Universe is watching out for you. Or maybe the Universe is forcing you in the direction of your true path. **The person who finally learns that the Universe is and has always been on their side can now take on exciting challenges once thought impossible!**

Action Plan

There's no better way to calm your emotions, organize your thoughts, rewire your neurological circuits, and formulate new ideas than journaling. Journaling is a cheap and effective form of therapy. When you write on paper or type on a computer, it's as if you're communicating with someone else even though your eyes will be the only ones that see the note.

Step 1
In no more than a page, no less than a few paragraphs, write your response to the scenario below.

Has anyone ever wronged you? Is there a specific experience or event that still causes you emotional stress? It could be anything or anyone. It could be a letter to THE UNIVERSE herself. Spend some time writing to whoever or whatever it is detailing how they wronged you and how they made you feel.

Step 2
When you're done, take the note and burn it! Watch it go in flames. Forgive them and wish them well. Where you're going, there's no place for hate or animosity. You are above that. The old you is gone, and the new you continues to emerge. You are becoming the best version of yourself.

Just a Thought

Abraham Lincoln once wrote a scathing letter to one of his generals for allowing Robert E. Lee to escape the Union forces after the Battle of Gettysburg. General Meade was given the orders to attack Lee when he was cornered, but instead, he held his forces back and let him go. Capturing Lee would have ended the war.

After Lincoln put the letter in an envelope and mailed it out, Lincoln immediately regretted sending the letter to General Meade, and he wished he could only have taken the letter back. In battle, while people are dying all around you and horrors are realized everywhere, attacking Lee was more easily said than done, and Lincoln knew this. Luckily, Mrs. Lincoln knew her husband would regret sending the letter, so she took it out of the mailbox before it was mailed out, and General Meade never saw it.[vii]

Oftentimes writing a letter to someone, or a tweet, or a text message, only to erase it before it's sent, satisfies the human psyche in a way sending the message could never have done.

SECRET #4:
The Power of Momentum

*A year from now the FUTURE YOU would have wished
you started today!*

On February 4, 2017, during Super Bowl 51, the Atlanta Falcons were destroying the New England Patriots. It was one of the most laughable Super Bowls on record, as the Falcons rode the momentum of their success to a 28–3 lead over the Patriots with most of the game over. Never in Super Bowl history had a team come back from this type of deficit, especially so late in the game. There was no way the Patriots and Tom Brady could come back from that much down— only a miracle could make that possible.

But, as we have said, miracles are the norm in life, not the exception. Tom Brady knows this! Tom has tapped into many secrets you are learning in this book. He understands that miracles are the norm, he knows the Universe is always on our side, he understands that state of mind matters more than circumstance, and if he didn't know already, he would soon find out that momentum can propel us to achieve what was thought to be impossible.

Midway through the third quarter, most New England fans probably went to sleep. The Patriots could not get anything going for themselves, and all seemed to be lost, but in sports, one play is all it takes to build momentum, and Tom Brady knew this. On what would be the most important play of the game, Tom Brady dropped back, and instead of throwing the ball or handing it off to a runner, he did something completely uncharacteristic—he decided to run the ball downfield himself, picking up a game-saving first down, which led to a touchdown, providing the spark needed to get the proverbial "ball rolling."

The New England Patriots' defense stopped the Atlanta Falcons on their very next possession. Tom Brady, riding the momentum of the defense, moved the ball downfield, scoring again. The offense rode the momentum of the defense, and the defense rode the momentum of the offense, and while Tom Brady and the Patriots scored possession after possession, the defense did not allow the Falcons to score at all. Before anyone could stop New England's momentum, the score was tied 28–28, and the game now moved into overtime. Riding this unbelievable momentum, the New England Patriots won the coin toss, received the ball, and scored a touchdown on the very first possession in overtime, capping the greatest comeback in NFL Super Bowl history.

Why does one person succeed while another fails? Why does one person become a multi-millionaire while another becomes homeless? Why does one person seem to have everything while another has nothing? The answer is that both of these people can actually be the same person, but what separates the two is that, often, the person who succeeds in life is the one who initially failed but persevered until they were able to harness the power of momentum and achieve stratospheric success. And it doesn't matter how far behind you are in life because one change can alter your momentum and skyrocket you towards greatness. The best part is the change you make doesn't have to be physical, it could be a simple change of perspective such as realizing that you're already a billionaire!

Failure is and always should be transitory, whereas success should be constant. You are only a failure if you settle for failing. Anthony Robbins, the great motivational speaker, was homeless and living in his car in his early twenties, but now he is worth nine figures. His protégé, Dean Graziosi, was labeled dyslexic, as well as struggled economically and academically, but he pushed past all his limitations and became a nationally bestselling author.

Secret #4 is that, by taking bold action in the direction of your dream or your passion, you initiate the power of momentum. Once momentum is activated, the energy generated from getting the "ball rolling" will take on a life of its own and propel you forward, without you having to do much more than just remain in an excited and positive state.

For example, when I was writing this book, the first sentence, the first paragraph, and the first page were the most difficult, but after I took the first step, it got easier, and before I knew it, I had hundreds of pages written. Most people never get the ball rolling because they think that whatever it is they believe they want to accomplish will be too difficult, but little do they know that the most difficult part is the first step, and after that, it gets easier. Why? Because you harness the power of momentum, and like a snowball rolling down a hill, the momentum picks up in speed and size with every revolution.

Again, this is not philosophy; it's physics. Very simply, an object at rest stays at rest, whereas an object in motion stays in motion until it's stopped. But when you are stopped, it's not an ending point—it's a road sign guiding you on your path.

To build momentum, you must take action, or at the very least, you have to take the first step in your desired direction. If you don't take the first step, you will never have a chance to accomplish your dream, but when you take a step in your desired direction, whatever that may be, you initiate the POWER OF MOMENTUM.

Alexander the Great

In 330 BC on the planes of Gaugamela in ancient Persia, located in modern-day Iraq, an army so vast that it drank the rivers dry and blocked out the sun with its arrows. This army, led by King Darius III of the Achaemenid dynasty, who controlled most of the known world, caused fear in all those who opposed it—except Alexander the Great.

The Persians were the most powerful kingdom at the time, since Greek states were always warring with each other, allowing the Persian empire to grow until it was at the height of its power and wealth. The Persian force of around 250,000 soldiers was made up of contingents from all districts loyal to Persia, known in ancient times as satrapies. Alexander's force was a contingent of Macedonian and allied Greek forces that was 5 times smaller than the Persian army, with no more than 50,000 soldiers.

How could Alexander challenge this enormous force? Why was he so confident? What did he know that everyone else did not?

At this time, for Alexander, money was running low, supply lines were constantly threatened, and lands that fell into the hands of the Greeks hung on by a thread, as almost every satrapy was at risk of rebellion. The only way Alexander could avoid disaster was if King Darius would face Alexander in battle, sooner rather than later, since a long, protracted stalemate would cause Alexander and his forces to run out of resources. Depletion of resources would cause dissent within his ranks and most likely end his invasion, but a final battle for the rule of the known world would allow Alexander to become king of all, overnight.

Even though Alexander and his invading force faced many challenges so far from home, he knew that if he was able to kill King Darius, the Persian army would collapse! Therefore, he didn't have to destroy an army of 250,000 soldiers, all he had to do was go "STRAIGHT FOR

THE KING" and kill the Persian King Darius in battle, which would leave the opposing army leaderless and force them to retreat.

So, a strategy was set up in which Alexander would lead a cavalry charge that would smash directly into Darius's forces, driving a wedge through the ranks of opposing soldiers. Alexander's army would then make their way to the noticeable King Darius, who was propped up on his 8-horse drawn chariot in splendid royal armor and surrounded by his 10,000 bodyguards, known as the immortals. The immortals were given this name because no matter what, the exact size of this force was always maintained, so if one soldier died, they were replaced immediately to keep the number at 10,000.

When the battle began, Darius launched most of his considerable force against the army of the Greeks while the Companion Cavalry led by Alexander, who was positioned at the apex of Wedge, riding on the back of his beautiful horse Bucephalus, launched straight into the forces of Darius. Could Alexander reach Darius before the Persians overwhelm the Greek forces?

Alexander was able to break through line after line of Persians using his daring cavalry charge in which the horses would ultimately run over the brave soldiers of the opposing army and send the "brave-less" scrambling, opening wider holes for more cavalry charges to break through the lines even further to get to King Darius.

Alexander came within a spear's throw of Darius, but before he could kill him, King Darius fled the field of battle. The Persian army was leaderless and forced to retreat, making Alexander the king of the known world.

Going Straight for the King

For thirty-six years, money seemed to always be flowing out of my hands. Whether it be paying for college, advanced degrees, a wedding, a home, cars, and everything else in between I never seemed to be able to accumulate true wealth. Anytime I extended myself financially, or whenever I entered the danger zone—the zone in which account balances were low and banks hit you with interest, strange fees, and fines—bad luck would soon follow. A tenant's check would bounce, an apartment building would spring a leak out of nowhere costing a fortune, and a low bank balance could turn into a negative bank balance very quickly compounding the pain.

Any extra money that I had would be used immediately to buy more assets or pay debts, keeping me at low balances. I constantly took enormous risks that quite often would come back to haunt me. There have been many times when I've looked back and said to myself, "Wow, if I'd just held on to that money, I would be in a great spot," or "If I'd just been patient, I would already be rich."

It wasn't until I sat down with my financial advisor and good friend Dominick Russo—the same Dominick from Chapter 3—that I learned to go straight for the king. Dominick taught me that creating a wealth account was the most important thing I could do financially, explaining that the account would accumulate over time and take the pressure off me mentally, freeing me up to think more clearly so that I could make more money. Also, if a once-in-a-lifetime opportunity came up, I, at the very least, could be in a position to capitalize on it. I said to myself, "No problem, let me give it a try." And the rest is history.

In addition to harnessing the power of momentum, sometimes we have to attack the one challenge in our lives that, if solved, will result in all other problems disappearing. This is what I refer to as **"going straight for the king."** Like Alexander the Great, when you go straight for the king, you forget about all your problems and all your distractions and all your obstacles, and you push forward until you overcome whatever it is that's been holding you back. When you do this, you not only initiate momentum, you become the momentum itself. You blast open a pathway for more opportunity and momentum to follow. You bend the will of the world in your direction by taking bold and assertive action in the direction of your greatest self.

Whether you're writing a book, creating a song, or opening a business, sometimes you have to focus and concentrate on one step at a time, but going straight for the king is the idea of taking multiple steps in your desired direction. For example, a person who is struggling financially may have a tough time going to school and paying for their PhD, but if they were able to get a scholarship or find a job that offers to pay for school, not only will they be able to take a step in their desired direction, but they will also be able to pay for school, "killing two birds with one stone."

Often, our one challenge is financial. Unfortunately, money happens to be very important in our society, as almost everything we do in life requires this resource. The idea is not to curse money or look at it as evil but instead to master it.

Imagine what you could do in life if you were financially independent, and you didn't have to worry about an erratic boss or an unscrupulous company for your financial survival?

I thought it was impossible—until I did it myself!

Through all my research, whether it be conversations with Bashar, or meetings with some of the most successful people in the world, a common theme appeared: "You can't save the world until you save yourself first." And more importantly, you don't have to save the world, all you need to do is be the best version of yourself, and you will then set an example for others to follow.

Creating and building a **GREATNESS** account is the first step in "saving yourself" so you can then have the time and money to save the world if you'd like.

What is a greatness account? It's an investment account or bank account that you build AUTOMATICALLY, paying yourself first before anything and anyone else, and never taking from it no matter what. What better way to prove to yourself that you are abundant than actually watching your account grow in size? There are financial instruments that allow you to borrow from your own account as if you are your own bank.

This may go against what so-called experts say about wealth creation, as many financial pundits advise to pay debt first. But what pundits fail to realize is that money is an energy force. The more you have, the more energy is stored and the more energy it attracts.

Warning: your greatness account should not be a bank account where you can withdraw money immediately like a bank or ATM. It must be an account that will take you a few extra steps and preferably a few extra days or weeks to access the money. This will prevent you from acting on any spending temptations you may have.

When you *begin* a greatness account, you let the Universe know that you are ready to *begin* accumulating wealth. Debts and low account balances repel money, whereas building a greatness account attracts it. Your greatness account can be one account or a combination of a few, but it should build money regardless of your financial situation, regardless of what's taking place around you financially. There are financial investments that offer you the ability to borrow money from the investment itself, but instead of paying a bank the interest payment, you pay yourself the interest, allowing you to become your own banker, instead of the borrower. This strategy is how you become financially independent and incredibly wealthy, but this topic is for another time, and perhaps even another book.

You will never get ahead if you pay everyone and everything first. This is a debt trap, a slave trap! **A MORTGAGE is "A DEATH PLEDGE"**; that's the true definition of the word. To get ahead, it is of the utmost importance to pay yourself first and pay yourself often. As soon as you begin to build this greatness account, you automatically let the Universe know that you are bypassing all the nonsense in your financial life by using a bold method of paying yourself, before anyone else, so that you accrue a level of personal wealth that #1 solves all of your problems and #2 keeps you in the state of being of abundance, which—as we have said—will attract to you more abundance!

Try it! Begin to pay yourself first. Start with $1 if you like, but the most important thing is to start NOW.

When I first began building my account, I started by automatically investing $50 a week. I did not notice if $50 a week went missing in my bank account, but within time, I watched as my account grew to a few hundred dollars. I decided to increase my investment from $50 a week to $100 a week, and within a few months, my account grew close to $1K. So then, I decided to invest $200 a week, because that's a dollar amount that wouldn't break the bank for me and wouldn't affect my life either way. Since my money was automatically purchasing investments that earned interest and income, my account started to grow to levels that were beginning to excite me.

Throughout my life, I was always carefree with my money. Like so many of us, spending brought me short-term happiness and blocked out my long-term stress and trauma. How was I ever going to be able to reverse this trend?

Once I began building my greatness account, I was finally motivated to become disciplined in my savings and even more disciplined in my spending. The feeling you get from this account building in size progressively overrides your temptation to waste money. It's as if the Universe was waiting for me to mature financially until it finally decided to provide me with true wealth and abundance.

Before long, I would invest upwards of $1,000 a week in this account because it became an obsession. Within time, my account rose to $10K, then $15K, then $20K, and that's when I truly started attracting money into my life without having to do anything.

I cannot chalk this up to coincidence because the only thing I did was build up my greatness account and my financial luck changed. NOTHING IN MY LIFE CHANGED! I still owed millions of dollars in debt, but I didn't care because I knew that I was on to something. I knew that I had tapped into a force that would help me attract all the necessary wealth I needed, and three years later, I had $0 in debt and over $1M in the bank.

Another way we can "go for the king" financially is simply to "pass go and collect $200." In the game Monopoly, if you make it around the entire game board and pass the spot on the board that says GO, which is the starting point, you collect $200 from "the bank." Once you've built up this money, without having to think much, you can start to build houses and hotels. Your wealth exponentially increases from there because another player has to pay you whenever they land on your property.

With that being said, building momentum financially does not require you to have a six- or seven-figure salary. I earned $55K a year as a NYC public school teacher when I started, but I saved and invested early on, and after three years of teaching, I purchased my first property. I was the worst stock trader in the world, and real estate offered me some type of control over my investment. I left teaching in 2016 and focused primarily on real estate, but if it wasn't for my teaching job,

I wouldn't have real estate. My teaching job was the equivalent of passing go and collecting $200.

Like I said, you don't need a high-paying job to start. You don't even need college. I'm not saying you shouldn't get a degree—I have a finance degree, an economics degree, and two master's degrees—but the most successful businessmen I know have no more than a few years of college between them. Can you believe that?

Unfortunately for me, I owed so much money in loans that not only did I have to teach during the day, but I taught after school, I taught night school, and I bartended on weekends. My cousin, in contrast, never went to college, became a sanitation worker for NYC, and with overtime, he made more money than anyone. He didn't owe student loans, and he wasn't foolish with his spending, so he was able to retire after twenty years of work. Now, at the age of forty-five, he can do whatever he wants in life.

The idea is that, if you can get a stable job that offers security without overwhelming responsibility, you can focus on other areas of your life to invest or to create. Passing go and collecting $200 is a strategy that can be used to get the ball rolling financially so that you can build momentum but still have time to add more value to humanity—or simply more money in your greatness account.

Attracting Wealth by Giving

When studying those who are enormously financially successful, a common theme emerges: giving money away. Remember, we have said that your state of being matters in attracting to you all that is representative of the energetic frequency you're giving off, so maybe the feeling we get from donating money automatically raises our frequency to put us in that peak state of abundance. I do believe so!

We have already said that giving gifts is a type of abundance, as it offers both the receiver and the giver a feeling of goodness. There seems to be an additional benefit to giving, which is that people who give more tend to receive more. It's as if, when we give to others, the Universe gives to us: "Give, and it shall be given unto you" (Luke 6:38).

What's the best way to give people money? Give anonymously, without them knowing the money came from you. You see, when someone receives a gift from you, the feeling you got from giving was your gift. If you give anonymously, the Universe seems to give you many multiples of the dollar amount you gave. This has happened in my life often, and the more generous I am, the more generous the Universe is regarding my finances.

Donate now, regardless of if you have money or not. Give a portion of your income to good causes or someone in need. Not only will it help someone else, but it will automatically put you in the peak state of abundance, which—as we have said—will attract to you more and more and more of it!

In Conclusion

Throughout history, by harnessing the power of momentum, wars were won, empires were built, dynasties were formed, temples were erected, roads were constructed, technology and medical breakthroughs were discovered, and humanity flourished.

I always believed that acting on my passion was an unrealistic way to make a living and that I needed to work an undesirable job and sacrifice my dreams to get rich. I was wrong! My passion paved the way to my greatest, most abundant life. Every great person I know followed their passion and mastered their reality in such magnificent ways. Maybe it's writing a song, creating a blog, or building a business that revolves around your passion; the idea is that acting on any one of your passions may provide you with all the momentum you need to create the greatest life possible. Simply by taking physical action, even if it's one step in the direction of our passion, we build that momentum we need, and we tap into a creative energy force that delivers the ideas and inspirations to help us bring our creation to fruition. Once you get the creative juices flowing, don't be surprised if you create something that opens the door to your greatest, most fulfilling life imaginable.

Harness the power of momentum by taking the first step in the direction of the most exciting thing you can think of. Then follow the synchronicities and coincidences as they guide you on your path. And if all seems to be falling apart around you, create your momentum by GOING STRAIGHT FOR THE KING!

I'll say it again: by taking physical action, we activate the force of momentum, and this is how you shatter limiting beliefs. This is how you discover your *true* purpose. This is how you find your *true* power. This is how you accomplish feats once thought impossible. This is how you become great!

Action Plan

Below are seven categories that, when given nourishment, will raise your vibration to that of a true life master and help you get the ball rolling on your path to greatness!

If there's a category you would like to add in addition to those below, then add it! Begin with one activity a day for each of the seven categories, but if you'd like to incorporate more than one in your daily routine, then do it!

Health   1.   2.   3.

Set three intentions that will boost your health, then act on them. You don't have to sign up to run a triathlon; anything that improves your physical or mental health will suffice.

1. Drink a glass of water in the morning.
2. Take a walk in nature.
3. Get fifteen minutes of sunlight.
4. Eat one serving of fruit and vegetables.
5. Do some light stretching.
6. Join a gym.
7. Sign up for a yoga, Pilates, or cycling class.

Abundance   1.   2.   3.

Set at least three intentions that will make you feel more abundant, then act on them. Remember, feeling abundant attracts more abundance.

1. Add money to your newly formed "greatness" account, even if it's a dollar. The idea is to get the ball rolling.
2. Give a gift to someone anonymously.
3. Pay off a bill that has been nagging your conscious and subconscious mind.
4. Volunteer your time.
5. Sell some of your old junk collecting dust and use that money to add to your "greatness" account.
6. Cancel unused subscriptions and add that money to your "greatness" account.

7. Create something, monetize it, and then add that money to your "greatness" account. You must be knowledgeable in something. If so, sell that knowledge.

Reading   1.   2.   3.

Reading has its own category. This also includes audiobooks or self-help videos you can listen to. I thought I was an avid reader because I read three books a month. That was until I discovered the greatness of audiobooks in which I still read three books, but I listen to another seven audiobooks. The most successful people throughout history were readers and lifelong learners. I use a timer when I read, and by the end of the month, I log the number of hours I read each month.

1. Read when you wake up and go to sleep. Start with ten minutes a day, then add as you go.
2. Read while you're waiting in a doctor's office or if you're waiting on hold on the telephone.
3. Listen to an audiobook on your way to work.
4. Listen to an audiobook while you're walking in nature.
5. Listen to an audiobook while you're taking a bath.
6. Read all different types of books on all different types of subjects.
7. Join a book club.

Meditation   1.   2.   3.

Set the intention to meditate each day. Perhaps the Universe has been waiting to communicate with you certain messages that will help you master life. Listen to what the Universe has to say, then act on it.

1. Learn how to meditate. Begin with a few minutes a day, then progress as you improve. You can download a meditation app or find free guided meditation videos on YouTube to get you started.

2. Walking, cycling, or any light, repetitive aerobic exercise gets the blood circulating throughout the body, which fuels the brain with oxygen-rich blood, putting us in a peak mental state of focus and concentration. You'll be surprised by the ideas and inspirations that flow through us when we are in an exercise-induced meditative state.

3. Keep a pad, pen, or some form of notetaker around so that when ideas flow through, you write them down. You'll be surprised at how many ideas flow through you when you become a conscious receiver of them.

4. Just by relaxing the jaw, focusing on the breath, and relaxing the body we get in a meditative state. This can be done anywhere, at any time. In fact, you can do it right now. Just drop the jaw, take a deep breath in through the nose, and relax the entire body as you exhale through the mouth.

5. Meditate when you're in the waiting room at a doctor's office. Meditate while you're on the phone and on hold. Meditate as often as possible.

6. Meditate by visualizing the future greatest version of yourself. Do this during a full moon and set the intention of becoming that version.

7. Meditate on any outcome you desire, focus on the outcome, and feel the emotion of that outcome coming

to fruition. Those who go on to achieve greatness use this type of mental conditioning to bend the will of the world in whatever direction they desire.

Overcoming Obstacles   1.   2.   3.

Do you have an unpaid bill or a deadline to meet? Make an intention to get it done. With each problem, challenge, or obstacle crossed off your to-do list, you can then add that energy back into your creative expression bank.

Every obstacle carries with it an energy that, if left to linger, can weigh down the physical mind. Just by attacking one obstacle a day you'll begin to feel lighter. That's what we call "enlightenment." When we feel lighter, we think more clearly, and when we think more clearly, we can solve problems more effectively. Then, before you know it, ideas and insights that were put on the back burner by the subconscious can now flow effortlessly to the conscious mind, and it's in this peak state that a magical idea can come forth, and when we act on that magic, greatness soon follows.

1. Pay that overdue bill, who, as we have said, "works for you and is your employee."

2. Create a to-do list and start hammering out each task, beginning with the easiest first. The idea is to build momentum.

3. With each task you complete, feel your physical energy field expand.

4. Clean and organize your room, your car, your paperwork, your emails. An organized environment helps clear the mind, and a clear mind leads to clear thoughts.

5. Regarding obstacles, visualize the outcome you desire, then attack each challenge with focused attention. Be on the lookout for wonderful lessons that can be learned in the process.

6. When you become a better version of yourself, you will begin to see problems as if you are a new person. Become the "new you" and solve the problems from the "new you" perspective. That "new you" will be able to overcome obstacles the "old you" struggled with.

7. Our greatest obstacles, trials, and tribulations can lead to our greatest victories. That is true greatness.

New Experiences   1.   2.   3.

Whether acting on a new creative endeavor, learning a skill, or traveling to a tropical island, new experiences stimulate our neural networks in such magical ways. One vacation, one new experience, one new relationship, one new book read, or one new skill learned can fulfill you in ways that cannot be quantified!

1. Book a vacation.

2. Learn a new skill. You can teach yourself how to sing or play piano in less time than you think. Just thirty minutes a day for a few weeks and you'll see improvement in these skills you never thought possible.

3. Travel a different way to work or school. Breaking up normal routines can promote alternate ways of thinking, and this can lead to new ideas and inspirations.

4. Take an online course based on your interests.

5. Sign up for a college class at your local school. Choose a subject that interests you.

6. Join a league that meets once a week. Possible recommendations could be bowling, basketball, softball, pickleball, bocce ball, or horseshoes. If you have physical limitations, then join a book club or a painting or pottery class.

7. Begin a new creative project. This is one of the best antidepressants available to humans. The Universe seems to reward us biologically when we follow our passions. Write a book, write a song, or create an online business.

"You Time"   1.   2.   3.

When was the last time you just relaxed in a bathtub, with no worries? When was the last time you took a "guilt-free" nap? When was the last time you spent the day doing absolutely nothing? Have you ever just turned your phone off with no care in the world? That is "you time" and you deserve it. In fact, the future you demands it!

1. Take a bubble bath and soak your troubles away!

2. Take a nap or sit on the couch and just rest.

3. Put your phone on "do not disturb" and leave it like that for good, or just turn off your phone without feeling any guilt at all!

4. Book a spa day for yourself. Get a massage, facial, or both.

5. Learn the word "no" and use it when people demand too much of your time! This category isn't named "their time." It's "you time."

6. Limit your time on social media as much as possible.

7. Celebrate the victories in your life as often as possible, guilt-free! When you overcome a challenge in your life, celebrate it. If this means going out and buying yourself an affordable gift, then do it. You don't have to spend money to celebrate. You can simply lie in a bubble bath or take a nap!

If we combine the first letters of each category word, we get the acronym HARMONY! This is no mistake! When our life is harmonious, our ability to focus and create is maximized! Your focus and your actions propel you to greatness!

SECRET #5:
Gratefulness is the Vibration of Greatness

"Act as if what you want to manifest has already manifested, give thanks, then allow The Universe to do the rest."

Seemingly out of nowhere, I woke up one morning with severe and sharp back pain that ran all down my legs. This was strange. I was in great shape physically, and I'd never felt this before. What in the world was going on?

My entire leg was beginning to go numb. You know the feeling you get when your leg falls asleep? For me, that feeling wouldn't go away. Knowing that physical activity was a very important aspect of my life, the fear of not being able to play sports, run, or even walk frightened me beyond belief.

After visiting an orthopedic doctor, surgery was recommended. A routine back surgery healed me, I was good as new, the numbness was gone, and I didn't even have to miss a day of work.

A few days after my back surgery, I limped into work, but little did I know that on this particular Friday, the 13th day in May, I would be in the middle of a student-on-student brawl. I had two choices, let the students kill each other or try to break it up before it escalated. I chose the second, but unfortunately one of the students snapped. I was unable to restrain the student, and before I knew what happened, the situation turned into a complete mess, which required security guards and deans from all over the school to intervene.

My surgery days prior all went for naught, as not only did I reinjure the area, but I had to go for emergency surgery so I could regain the feeling in my legs. I spent the next few months urinating in bed without being able to control it. What were the odds of this "unusual situation" happening days after my surgery?

When I finally got my head together a few months later, I started to think the Universe had different plans for me. Luckily, I never missed work and had many unused sick days that accumulated throughout the years because as soon as those sick days ran out, the Department of Education cut me off. In addition, I always had multiple income streams coming in to support me so that if anything happened with one income stream, I could always rely on another. I was also able to restructure several investments I had and refinance a large loan that would support me until I got back on my feet—literally.

It wasn't until I showed gratitude that all started to fall into place. For the first time in a very long time, I was able to sit back and look at my life from a different point of view. I began meditating, reading, learning, and doing things I'd never had time to do before my injury. My investments and multiple income streams not only saved me, but they also allowed me to leave teaching for good. Many of the financial moves I made never would have been made had I not been injured. Many of these secrets in this book would also not have been learned had I not been injured. Miracles that I'd never had time to pay attention to would not have been noticed had I not been injured. Poof, within moments my entire life changed, and in the end, it all seemed to be a blessing that was initially disguised as a nightmare.

Once I realized miracles were the norm in life, that the Universe was conspiring in my favor, and that my reaction to circumstances was more important than the circumstance itself, gratefulness became my new state of being, and more things to be grateful for began to appear. And just like that, I discovered another piece of the divinely orchestrated puzzle of existence, proving to me, beyond a shadow of a doubt, that a higher power exists, and it can be accessed simply by being grateful.

If nothing seems to be going right in our lives, the quickest way to reverse this trend is to focus on the things that *are* going right. Most of us live an ungrateful life, creating a repellent for the great things in life to find us. Why should the Universe give us anything when we're not grateful for what we already have been given?

This is Secret #5: showing gratitude for what we already have will help us attract that which we desire.

Even though there are so many things to be grateful for, most people, including me, only notice the things we don't have. But if we were to lose something that's dear and precious to us, we would then desire that loss as if it were a pot of gold.

Start practicing the art of gratitude by focusing on that which you already have. Maybe it's your spouse, your children, your job, your health, your family's health. Maybe it's the idea that you have eyes to see or ears to hear or feet to walk or hands to hold things. Maybe, just maybe, it's as simple as feeling the warm sun on your skin on a beautiful summer day or the feeling you get while watching a sunrise or a sunset. You see, there's beauty all around us, we are quite abundant, and we have so much in life to be grateful for.

Being grateful is one of the greatest gifts we can give the Universe, and as soon as we show gratitude, the Universe seems to find a way to give us more to be grateful for. **It's as if the invisible force that guides all things waits for us to be grateful for what we already have before providing us with more of what we desire.** Think about that! Would you rather give a gift to someone who's appreciative or a person who couldn't care less? And if you didn't receive something

THE 7 SECRETS OF GREATNESS

from the Universe, then it wasn't time to receive it because something better is waiting to be delivered to you.

If you insist on wanting anything, it would be wise to want what you truly need, as the higher mind, the Universe, and all of creation know what's best for us and therefore do not necessarily take into consideration our wants, unless what we want is truly what we need.

When our needs become our wants, we override the Matrix programming! When our needs become our wants, we signal to the Universe that we are no longer trapped, and we are now ready for greatness! When our needs become our wants, not only does an angel get its wings, but a demon loses theirs!

I can tell you from firsthand experience that being in a state of gratitude can lift you out of the darkest recesses of hell. There isn't a more powerful way to get into the vibration of abundance and greatness than to focus on gratitude, and for many people, just turning on the "gratitude switch" is all they need to do to begin to master life.

Manifesting Through Gratitude

It's the people who aren't afraid to do the impossible who actually achieve it!

Greg Braden is an author, a scientist, and an educator, who has appeared on the widely popular show *Ancient Aliens* and who has created his television series *Missing Links*. By helping us expand our consciousness and think outside the box, Braden has been at the forefront of helping humanity achieve its highest potential.

In episode 7 of *Missing Links*, Greg Braden tells the story of how his Native American friend called and asked him if he would be kind enough to "pray for rain with him." The phone call came during a time of "one of the worst droughts in the history of the American

Southwest," which greatly affected agriculture in New Mexico. Braden agreed to meet with his indigenous friend at the specified time, date, and place.

They hiked over 130K acres, seeing "some of the most beautiful high-altitude sage you could imagine," before coming to a circular rock formation with a 25-foot diameter. The rock formation was referred to as a "medicine wheel," which had been maintained for generations by the ancestors of Braden's indigenous friend. Braden asked, "Why is this location so special?" And his friend replied, "This is a place where the skin between the worlds is very thin."

Greg Braden said, "My indigenous friend unlaced the shoes of his old work boots, and he stepped barefoot into the medicine wheel. He closed his eyes and created a prayer in front of me for a few seconds. He then turned around and looked at me, and he said, 'I'm hungry. Want to go for lunch?' I said, 'Sure, we can go for lunch, but I thought you invited me here to pray for rain?' This is when he turned and looked at me, and what he said changed my life; it changed my perspective and the way I think about my relationship to the world. He said, 'No, I didn't pray for rain.' He said, 'If I prayed for rain, the rain could never happen. Because the moment we ask for something to happen, in asking for it, we are affirming that it does not exist now. In other words, when we ask the Universe for something, we are implying that whatever we are asking for, whatever we are trying to manifest, whatever we want to appear, is not present at that moment, and in that way, we are actually affirming, in the quantum field, the very thing that we were hoping to change.' So I asked my friend, 'Well, if you didn't pray for rain, what did you pray for?' He replied, 'When I closed my eyes, I felt the feeling as if the rain had already happened. I felt the feeling of what it feels like to stand in my pueblo village with my naked feet in the mud, and the mud is there because there's been so much rain. I smelled the smells of what it smells like when the rain rolls off the earth and walls of our pueblo homes. I felt the feeling of what I feel like when I walk across the corn fields that have grown past my chest because there has been so much rain.' He said, 'I felt the feeling of what it feels like when my prayer is already answered, and then I give thanks for what has already happened.' And in those few seconds, he felt the feelings and gave thanks to all that has already occurred."

After Greg and his friend ate lunch, large black storm clouds were seen forming overhead and that part of New Mexico received more rain that day than in the past five years. The local weathermen on television were unable to explain the unique pressure drop in the system of New Mexico that day.[viii]

The Key to Manifestation

Wanting is its own unique state of being. When we want something, we're effectively saying we don't have it. In other words, wanting is not having; wanting something merely keeps us in a state of wanting and not having. **The key to manifesting the life of your dreams is to be in a state whereby, through visualization, you can picture whatever it is that you desire. Instead of wanting this or that, you know that you already have it, and you give thanks to the Universe for receiving it, allowing it to manifest.**

This does not mean that we should not have any wants. It's just that the Universe seems to manifest for us whatever it is that we are constantly thinking of or focusing on currently in our lives. So, if we're focusing on "not having," the Universe will oblige and produce for us the reality that is consistent with this feeling of lack, but on the other hand, if we think and focus on the idea that we are abundant, and we remain in a positive state, the Universe will have no other choice but to manifest this reality in our life.

Giving puts us in the vibration of having. We can't give what we don't have. So, by giving, we convey the message to the Universe that we have, and by having, we prove we are abundant!

While in the state of having, which is another term for a state of abundance and gratitude, we may find that a job opportunity comes our way, an idea springs up out of nowhere, or we may meet someone that lights up our life, and don't be surprised if money starts to appear in such extraordinary and magical ways!

You don't have to learn to be in the vibration of manifestation to attract what you need. You're already giving off that core frequency. That's your true, essential self. All you have to do is get out of the way of the vibration that you're giving off, and then you will attract everything you need by letting go of beliefs that are obscuring that vibration. –Bashar

Bashar—the Sixth Form of Abundance

We have previously mentioned five forms of abundance: (1) money, (2) trade and barter, (3) gift-giving and -receiving, (4) synchronicity, and (5) ideas and inspirations that will support you on your path to greatness. But there is a sixth; and so important is this skill that Bashar requested it be included in this book. Think of this skill as a master key that opens the door to all other forms of abundance. Some are born with this ability; some learn it later in life; some wield it with care, and others wield it for manipulation; however, those who fail to learn this form of abundance will often work for those who have mastered it. The sixth form of abundance is **communication**.

Shortly after graduating college, I went to work on Wall Street, and it was here where I would encounter one of the greatest communicators and leaders of men I had ever come across. A simple five-minute pep talk from this man would have an entire office erupt in cheer and celebration as if we'd won some kind of championship. The reason he was a tremendous leader was because he was a tremendous communicator; and so fascinating was this ability he wielded that it's no surprise this man is now a billionaire.

Your ability to communicate effectively will get you that job; it will get you that promotion; it will win you friends; it will disarm your enemies; and oftentimes it will get you out of sticky situations. But most of all, learning this skill will give you a serious advantage in every aspect of your life. The best part about communication is that it can be learned; it can be improved; it can be mastered and wielded with great effect to bring you more abundance.

People like Alexander the Great, Julius Caesar, and Abraham Lincoln were the greatest leaders of their time because they were the greatest communicators of their time. Warren Buffet, one of the richest men in the world, was scared to death of public speaking, but he knew he had to master this ability to become what he is today. No matter what you do in life, be it a coach, a businessman, a teacher, or a parent, as soon as you improve your communication skills, every area of your life is elevated. And it's not just you who benefits from this skill—all those fortunate enough to listen to you may also benefit, as I have under great communicators.

When studying the lives of great leaders and their ability to communicate effectively, a common theme emerges. The best communicators speak from the heart because in doing so, they speak directly to the heart of the listener, and words seem to be magnified by the integrity, honesty, and truthfulness that comes from this type of message. When we hear others speak from the heart, with no ulterior motive other than what is best for all parties listening, that message is felt in a special kind of way, like a beautiful song or poem. And there's no better communicator in the world today than Bashar, who not only speaks from the heart, but speaks from the soul, and in doing so he is able to wield his message like a sword, helping his listeners cut a path to their greater selves.

When you speak truth, and when you begin to live a life more representative of your truest self, don't be surprised if you begin to spot deception and lies more easily. It's almost as if we become our own little human lie detectors once we begin to dabble in the art of truthfulness.

Communication is not limited to just speaking. Art, music, writing, designing, decorating, or anything that helps us express ourselves can be considered communication. Sometimes the best way to communicate is to just be silent and listen because you never know when an awe-inspiring idea or some insight will come from a random conversation, as this has happened to me so often in my life. From now on, any person I have a conversation with, whether it be the CEO of a Fortune 500 company or a homeless man on the street, I listen attentively because they may be able to provide me with the exact information I was looking for to help me overcome a challenge or to help me improve my life in some way. I do not believe random conversations to be random at all. I believe them to be divinely orchestrated like so much of our reality.

Mastering our Words

The words we use offer others a peek into our innermost thoughts and feelings.

Words can start or end wars; words can build a person up or tear them down; words can unite or divide us, changing the course of history.

When carefully placed, words support each other like good comrades, picking each other up where one may fall to create meanings, definitions, and explanations of our innermost feelings and ideas. Words affect our thoughts, our emotions, and our actions. Words spoken to another person force us to take responsibility for what we're saying. And even if we doubt what we're saying, words have a funny way of tricking us into believing in them. If there's a goal you want to accomplish, tell someone about it because it adds an extra level of motivation to the accomplishment, and since the pain of failing will be compounded by the pain of dishonoring yourself in the eyes of another, you will be doubly motivated to act.

Magicians cast spells using words. Perhaps that's why they call it spelling. The greatest professional athletes in history like Larry Bird and Michael Jordan used words as psychological swords to cripple the psyche of opposing players. Words overwrite memory; it's the reason pathological liars begin to believe their own words; it's why those who practice positive affirmations like "I am abundant," "I am grateful," or "I am powerful" report magical, empowering effects. **What you say becomes so; so, watch what you say!**

This is how important words are. They are not words; they are vibrational sounds that dance with universal energies and can be used to encourage, support, or motivate all who have the pleasure of hearing them. Choose them carefully; choose them wisely; choose them positively.

The words we use can literally change our lives overnight, for the good or the bad! For instance, when we use self-motivated talk, we send a signal to the Universe that we intend a specific outcome. When we do this with confidence and conviction, we allow the subconscious mind to process the verbal self-talk and provide us with all the biochemical and neurological responses and support for us to physically and mentally get the job done.

This may take practice, as you may be conditioned to use words negatively. Break the habit. Break the momentum. If you belittle someone, you not only lower the vibration of the person to whom your words were directed, but you also lower your vibration.

Conversely, when you sincerely compliment someone, both of your vibrations are raised. A compliment can light up another person's life, allowing them to shine their light brighter, and when you magnify another person's light, you magnify your own. A compliment can have long-lasting effects, and what better gift to give someone than a gift that keeps on giving? A compliment can change a person's life, and that can change the world!

When we become generally interested in what someone has to say, we become a better communicator. When we listen attentively instead of talking, we become a better communicator. Something as simple as smiling or remembering someone's name makes us a better communicator. Empathy, seeing things from another's perspective, is not only the foundation of great communication but also the hallmark of great leadership. If you were in someone else's shoes and lived the life they lived and went through the trials and tribulations they have, you, too, may see the world just like they do. So be kind, be understanding, be tolerant, see things from others' perspectives, and be grateful that others are different from you because their differences define you, just as the dark defines the light.

Guides of Greatness

I remember the day perfectly. It was the first day of school upon entering the third grade. I cried my eyes out from the minute I woke up that day to the moment I stepped into the schoolyard. I held on to my mom as tight as possible. I didn't want to let her go. I was scared to death. In fact, I would have rather died that day than gone to school, so I held on to my mom as if my life depended on it and begged her to please take me home.

While in front of the school, a young boy walked up to me and said "There's nothing to be scared of. I'll walk you in." And this fearless young boy grabbed my hand and walked me into school that day, and we became the best of friends. I had no more fear.

I would go on to learn so much from this kid growing up. He was made of something different. He never missed a day of school. He succeeded in everything he did. A fascinating force of nature this young boy was.

Unfortunately, we wound up going to different high schools, and where I would fall apart time and time again, this young man continued to excel academically. Upon graduation, he attended the prestigious West Point Academy. Later, he served our American forces as a high-ranking officer in Iraq and Kosovo, returning home as a hero. He would go on to work for Goldman Sachs and then was recruited by a gentleman Vincent Viola, a legendary New York mercantile exchange trader who would later purchase the NHL Florida Panthers.

With that being said, Mr. Viola made the wise decision to hire my friend to work for him. This man who had so courageously walked me into school as a boy was given the position of president and CEO of the Florida Panthers hockey team. And now Matthew Caldwell is one of the top executives in all of sports.

While writing this book, to show you that miracles are the norm, Matthew and the Florida Panthers, on their way to the Stanley Cup Finals, pulled off one of the greatest upsets in sports history, coming back from a 3–1 deficit to beat the number-one-seeded Boston Bruins. This was no ordinary team the Florida Panthers beat; the Bruins were arguably one of the best teams ever, winning more games than any other team in regular season history.[ix] That's a miracle!

Just like in the example of major league baseball star Jason Marquis, people like Matthew Caldwell are way-showers. They are guides and beacons of hope because they pave the path for others to follow in their footsteps, and all those who were lucky enough to know them are motivated to strive for a level of excellence already attained by these amazing individuals.

Grateful is an understatement! I am truly blessed that the Universe has given me a front-row seat to some of the most successful people in the world, and I can't help but think that this was done on purpose. After studying these great people, I can tell you that they all have one thing in common, and that is that they have such mastery of their inner world. So much so that their outer world has no other choice but to mirror the confidence and greatness they feel inside.

These guides should never be envied; they should be emulated because they set a high bar for excellence and challenge all those around them to rise and meet it. In other words, they show us what can be possible! They show us the way!

Who in life are your "guides of greatness"?

In Conclusion

As we open to the idea that we are quite abundant, and once we allow other forms of abundance to enter into our lives, it's the state of gratitude that will bring us even more abundance. This is how people truly master life!

Being grateful is another link in the chain of greatness, and like a magnet, this energetic frequency attracts to us luck, opportunities, and many other positive things that we might have previously thought were out of reach.

Gratitude removes the negative frequencies that interfere with your peak state of being so you can begin to operate on a superhuman level. Gratitude isn't a passive emotion; it's a complete knowingness that no matter what happens in this world, it's the greatest thing that ever could have happened, and by knowing this, you are so grateful to be a part of it all. It's an empowering and energizing force. It quells sadness, destroys depression, slays anger, quiets doubt, feeds joy, and is a very simple step we can take in the direction of true happiness and fulfillment.

Gratefulness is the vibration of greatness!

The best part is you don't need to wait for outside forces to control your happiness—just smile and be grateful. Remember, the reflection in the mirror doesn't change until we change! Since communication is a sixth form of abundance, and the *WORDS* we use daily are a reflection of our beliefs, thoughts, and emotions, our ability to wield them with care will propel us rapidly on the path to greatness.

Gratitude is how we should start the day; it's how we should end the day; it's how we should pray; and it's how we should live our lives from moment to moment!

Action Plan

1. Compliment one person each day.

Have you ever been complimented?

There've been instances where one compliment prevented someone from taking their own life—think about what would happen in the world if we complimented rather than criticized each other! One compliment can change your entire mood; it can maybe even change your entire world!

Practice complimenting at least one person each day, but the more the merrier. The Universe could always use more complimenters and fewer criticizers!

2. Write five positive things.

In addition to complimenting one person a day, each night before you go to bed, write down at least five positive things you're grateful for. Things you saw, heard, experienced, or accomplished that day.

Maybe you complimented someone, or they complimented you. Maybe you helped someone in need, and it made you feel good. If so, write it down. If you aced an exam, write it down. If you went to the gym, write it down. If you learned a new skill, write it down.

When we focus on gratefulness, we train the mind to think in a certain way, and for some who are new to this, it can have the added effect of rewiring their neurological circuits, creating a newer and better version of themselves.

Get in the habit of being grateful by doing this exercise for at least ten days, and don't be surprised if the Universe provides you with more to be grateful for.

Example:

	Monday	Tuesday	Wednesday	Thursday	Friday	Saturday	Sunday
1.	Went to a Yoga & Pilates class						
2.	Received a compliment from a stranger						
3.	Learned something new						
4.	Read for thirty minutes						
5.	Meditated for ten minutes						

SECRET #6:
The Journey Is the Destination

The unknown is where "THE GREATEST YOU" exists!

He knew success like no other. He played in two Super Bowls, became an NFL Hall-of-Famer, and even appeared in a baseball World Series. As a two-sport professional athlete, this man had money, cars, homes, and a family; he had everything. A life one can only dream of. He succeeded at the highest levels of human achievement, but in 1997, at the height of his success, this man would attempt suicide by driving off a forty-foot cliff. He survived without sustaining any significant injuries, and it was at this time that Deion Sanders realized his life was worth living. It was at this time that Sanders dug down deep and found something in him that was missing. He found his true self.[x]

Sanders's true mission in life may not have been playing sports; perhaps it was helping people. After retiring from football and baseball, Sanders became a minister, a coach, and a mentor to current and former professional athletes. Today, Sanders is one of the most highly sought-after football coaches in college football after winning the Eddie Robinson Coach of the Year Award at Jackson State University in 2021.

How can someone with seemingly everything going for them feel so empty inside?

You have heard the saying, "If you don't know where you're going, how will you know when you get there?" Many people look for a final destination point in their journey, but once that point is reached, they somehow feel unfulfilled and look for another destination point. What people fail to realize is that the journey *is* the destination.

This is Secret #6: The journey is the destination, the path is the process, the experience itself is the goal, and wisdom gained is the gift. All the good stuff, all the bad, all the highs, all the lows help guide us and help mold us so that we can become the best us, the true us, the wise us, the great us!

> *If you're focusing to some degree on a goal, that is fine, but the idea is to just be in the journey and value the process. Enjoy what you're doing for its own sake. You don't have to accomplish anything, because the "doing of what you enjoy" is the accomplishment. Yes, that's enough. So, if you just do what you enjoy, you have already created the idea of accomplishment and success, and all of the rest of it is just needless expectation. The so-called goal is just the side effect and representation of whatever happens when you follow your own joy and creativity. A goal is not the achievement of a particular outcome; it's just the expression of what you've already achieved by just doing what excites you because you don't need another reason.*
> *—Bashar*

Finding the Right Path

We've been programmed to believe that to become successful or to make as much money as possible, we must go to college, get a degree, and then go work for a prestigious company, but I can tell you that's not true at all. In fact, the most successful people I know didn't graduate college, instead using those years to build businesses and follow their dreams.

While I was slaving away in college, Jason Marquis was pitching in the World Series. It was only after he followed his dream of playing in the majors that he went back to school to receive a degree. Another friend of mine forwent college completely and became one of the most successful landscapers in NYC. Another friend of mine left college in his first year, only to become a multi-millionaire entrepreneur.

Other notable people who left school early or forwent it completely:[xi]

1. Steve Jobs, Founder of Apple, dropped out of college after one semester.

2. Mark Zuckerberg, co-founder of Facebook, dropped out of college in 2005 to focus on his social media platform.

3. Paul Allen, the billionaire co-founder of Microsoft, dropped out of college.

4. Rachel Ray, celebrity chef and businesswoman, dropped out of college after two years.

5. Jack Dorsey, CEO of Twitter, dropped out of college twice.

6. David Neelman, CEO and founder of JetBlue, dropped out of college.

7. Presidents William McKinley and Harry Truman dropped out of college.

8. Real estate developer R. Donald Peebles, one of Forbes's listed wealthy African Americans, dropped out of school to get his real estate license. He is worth over $700M.

9. H. Wayne Huizenga, who built up Blockbuster and owned three sports franchises, including the Miami Dolphins, dropped out of college.

10. Ty Warner, the billionaire behind the idea of Beanie Babies, dropped out of college in the '60s.

11. Tech mogul Michael Dell, founder of Dell Computers, dropped out of college after two years.

12. Larry Ellison, CEO of Oracle and one of the richest men in the world, worth $135B, dropped out of college his sophomore year because his adoptive mother passed away.

13. Oprah Winfrey would leave school early to pursue a career in media, only to graduate thirteen years later.

14. Steve Wozniak, famous Apple engineer and pal of Steve Jobs, planned to take a 1-year break from college, but that year would last over a decade.

15. Henry Ford, owner and creator of the Ford Motor Company, never went to college. Instead, he moved to Detroit, Michigan, to work as an apprentice.

I could go on and on with this list, but you get the idea. The point I'm trying to make is that your journey does not have to conform to the ideas and expectations of everyone else's journey. A person who does what they love to do daily does not have to work a day in their life. **That's true success, not what we've been conditioned to believe.**

We are always on "the right path" because we are the path. You will know if you divert from your path; it's no more complicated than that. So, if you want some sort of a litmus test, as you say, all you have to do is ask yourself the question: ***am I acting on my highest excitement every moment that I*** *possibly can, to the best of my ability, with no insistence on a particular outcome? The answer is either yes or no. That will give you the ability to then ask the next question: if you're not, then why?*

Examine the beliefs that would make it seem logical not to be who you really prefer to be, and then you can let go of those beliefs that don't serve you. You can know that, having discovered those beliefs that are not necessarily part of who you are, that's still part of your path because your life is a process. That's the point—you discover more of who you are from a different point of view, a different perspective, so even when you discover things on your path that you don't prefer, discovering them is part of your path. You can't really be on the wrong path in life.

—Bashar

Everybody's journey is different; what works for one person may not work for another. As we have said, if you get a simple job that allows you to "pass go and collect $200" *but still offers you the freedom to create,* you can make more money than doctors who went to school for many years and probably owe tons of money in student loans. I know people who are firemen, cops, sanitation workers, and teachers who own their own businesses on the side and make millions.

The person who has the time to do what they truly love to do in this world is the real success, not the one who works fourteen hours a day in a cubicle or in front of a computer without any free time. **Reminder:** the "pass go and collect $200" strategy should be a job that does not monopolize (pun intended) all your time and energy, as that will hurt your ability to create. Do not quit your day job until you truly believe what you're doing is going to support you. As Bashar says, "Don't jump off a cliff without a parachute."

Passing the Failure Test

Queen, like most bands, struggled early on in their career.[xii] The band signed with a production company but was only given studio time during off hours when the studio was empty, which was usually in the middle of the night. They spent their time giving free concerts to their friends and taking whatever odd gig they could book, playing to empty halls and crowds of very few.

The band's guitarist, Brian May, said that during one gig, "when we were due to go back on for the second half, the lady who was the chairman of events came up to us in the middle of the interval and said, 'Um, really good, boys. We had a request.' We said, 'Oh yeah, what was the request?' She said, 'The people would like to have the disco in the second half instead of you guys.' So, we said, 'Fine,' and she gave us the 20 pounds. But that was a blow to our confidence."

Finally, after a year their first album was released, but in the words of drummer Roger Taylor, "the album resoundingly flopped." Working hours and hours, and spending about three times the budget, Queen finished a second album, and then a third album soon followed, but the band really struggled financially at this time. "The managers were building swimming pools and driving Rolls Royces" while the band was making something like 20 pounds a week ($26 US dollars).

Queen would later sign on with another management team, and their 20-pound-a-week payment was raised to 30 a week. Still struggling, it was now "do or die" because if their next album flopped, it could have very well been their last.

Here's where Queen's story ties into many of the Secrets in this book. This fourth album, *Night at the Opera*, is where Queen went straight for the king: all four members of the band forgot about the obstacles and distractions in their lives and focused on creating the best album they could create. The beauty of this album is that Queen was given carte blanche to write whatever songs they wanted, and this newfound excitement opened up pathways of creativity that changed the entire landscape of music shortly after this album was created. This is also when Freddie Mercury tapped into the miracle force and created what is known to be one the best rock and roll songs of all time: "Bohemian Rhapsody."

In the end, the album was a huge success, and the song "Bohemian Rhapsody" took on a life of its own. Riding this momentum, and remaining in a positive state of mind, Queen wrote hit after hit, and the rest is history. Years later, they are still highly regarded as one of the best, if not the best, bands of all time. They went from playing in front of a crowd of three people to playing in stadiums with over 90K swarming fans singing along to their hits because THEY NEVER QUIT!

There's one characteristic commonly shared by many people who have succeeded, and that's the ability to fail consistently without giving up. **Think of failure as nothing more than the Universe testing you to see if you can truly handle success.** In failure, there's knowledge, there's learning, there's wisdom. In addition to teaching us valuable lessons, failure has the ability to guide us to a different path—in many cases, a better path.

It's as if the Universe knocks us down continuously to see if we are worthy of receiving something great. It's as if, as soon as we prove ourselves to the Universe, success becomes the norm, and we can go on and accomplish feats we never thought were possible.

Do you think Queen knew they were going to be the best band of all time? They were close to having to call it quits, but they didn't, and the rest is history. **The more the Universe knocks you down, the greater the prize at the other end.**

Begin with the End in Mind

Picture walking into a funeral parlor. You see people dressed in black, spread out all over the room, some crying, some talking in groups remembering the life and times of the person who just passed away. You continue to hear tearful cries and see tear-soaked handkerchiefs being used by certain people you remember well. In the back of the room, you see a casket, surrounded by wall-to-wall flowers and picture collages.

Everyone is asked to sit down, and as you take your seat, someone close to you walks to the podium to deliver the eulogy. You decide to stand up and peek into the casket to see who died, and when you do, you realize that IT IS YOU! This is your funeral. Now, the person at the podium, who knew you most, begins to speak about your life.

In *The 7 Habits of Highly Effective People*, Stephen Covey describes a technique—or what he refers to as a habit—that challenges the reader to think about their life "beginning with the end in mind." In other words, the reader will recreate their own life story beginning from the day they die and ending at the present day. This is a eulogy from the point of view of someone who is still alive and knew them intimately.[xiii]

"According to Covey, before you can live a good, meaningful life, you've got to know what that looks like. When we know how we want people to talk about us at the end of our life, we can start taking action NOW, to make that scenario a reality later. With the end in mind, we'll know what we need to do day to day and week to week to get there."[xiv]

How would you like to live? How would you like to be remembered?

> **Bashar on Living in the Moment:**
>
> *When you follow your passion, when you live in the moment, and when you no longer have the impulse to chase the person that is no longer you, that is when everything changes.* So, sometimes you need to stay where you are! Remember, if you don't stay where you **actually** are, then nothing that you **actually** want can find you because you're not home, and you only exist here and now. But when you create the illusion of focusing on the past, focusing on the future, worrying about this, worrying about that, that which could come to you naturally and effortlessly has no place to anchor because you're not home. Sometimes, all you need to do is stay home and everything will come to your home by doing the things, by taking the actions that are truly representative of who you really are. Everything that happens in the next moment is exactly what needs to happen, and if you treat it that way and respond to it that way, everything else falls into place automatically. Then, it's home sweet home.

In Conclusion

Our experiences in life offer us the ability to gain wisdom, grow spiritually, and learn lifelong lessons, which make us the unique people we are today. The journey is what defines us!

If enemies attack us, if so-called "bad things" happen to us, if pain and suffering creep into our lives, just know that we are strengthened by each and every experience—the good and especially the bad. Often, the darkness in our lives prepares us, strengthens us, and helps us grow even more so than if everything was love and light. If life was just "cupcakes" and "rainbows," would you truly value the good times, or would you just take them for granted? It's the challenges, the obstacles, and the failures that humble us, that keep us balanced, that keep us grounded.

The real heroes in life are the people who overcome addiction, or recover from a bankruptcy, or suffer a letdown but eventually pick themselves up. They are the people who turn the ship around and succeed. The people who find their way through the darkness and show others the way to the light.

Action Plan

Now that you've gotten the picture and the feeling of your funeral, it's time for you to create your eulogy. Think about the best life you could have lived and write it down.

In no less than two paragraphs, write your eulogy from the point of view of a cherished friend or a loved one who knew your entire life story. What would you want this person to say about the life you lived? What were your accomplishments? What were your memorable moments? What do you want people to say about you? How do you want to be remembered?

This is a very powerful exercise; it truly motivated me to take responsibility for my life now so that I don't have any regrets before I die. Save this eulogy as a reference and come back to it in time to review it. Let it motivate you to accomplish your dream life.

SECRET #7:
The Formula

Excitement is the fuel required to create the life of our dreams, achieve the impossible, or both.

At a certain point in my life, real estate became my highest excitement. It was my joy; it was my passion. One day, when I first began to invest in properties, I went to a free Robert Kiyosaki Real Estate seminar. I came a little late, and it was packed, but luckily there were two seats open, one for me and one for the guest who came with me.

Mr. Kiyosaki was brilliant and mesmerizing as he delivered such valuable information in that seminar, but the real benefit came from the person I met who happened to be sitting next to me. This wonderful person whom I had just met and I spoke for an hour after the seminar and exchanged numbers. He was an experienced investor, and he offered to share some ideas with me. He did this not out of a desire for profit but because he truly wanted to help.

He invested in apartment buildings in and around NYC, and the information I gained from this individual was life-changing, because within three years, I too would be an investor in apartment buildings in the same locations. He drove with me to these locations and helped me choose my first building. We shared ideas, and we helped and supported each other along the way. I look back at the day of that seminar and wonder, *What would my life be like if I had stayed home?*

At the time, I could not think of anything more exciting than seeing Robert Kiyosaki. I followed my excitement and took action by physically going to the seminar. Then I allowed synchronicity to guide me by finding the last two seats in the seminar, which happened to sit me next to a person who just so happened to change my life.

When I look back at every turning point in my life, there are moments when I could have turned left instead of right, or I could have stayed in my house instead of going out, and that decision would have changed my life entirely. For the rest of your lives, whenever you make a decision, choose the one that contains the most excitement. That's the direction that is being communicated to you by the higher mind. That is the direction you should follow.

Secret #7 is that our highest potential can be achieved when we're in a state of excitement. This is the one secret that rules all other Secrets because if we discover our excitement and act on it, all other Secrets found in this book will fall into place. Excitement is the path that leads to our *divine purpose* and our *divine purpose* is the path that leads to our greatest life!

What if I told you that there was a simple formula that, when applied, will allow you to take control of your life immediately so that you can truly master "the Matrix"? A formula that incorporates the six Secrets previously learned in this book and combines them with your creativity to help you reach your true potential and construct the perfect life for you? A formula so simple, so obvious, hidden in plain sight, patiently waiting to be rediscovered?

As children, we understood the concept, but as we grew older, most of us lost sight of it because many of the belief systems we picked up along the way have blinded us. I am not here to teach you "the

Formula"—you already know it. I am here to help you remember it so that you can reapply it and then live the life you were born to live, so you can be the person you were born to be.

I wish I could take credit for *the Formula*, but I cannot; the only thing I can take credit for is that, whenever I or anyone I knew applied it in their life—both knowingly and unknowingly—it worked. Whether it is my good friend and mentor the great Billy Carson, a multiple best-selling author, the CEO of 4Bidden Knowledge, owner of his own television network, and who, by following his passion, has awoken millions and millions across this planet; or my former student Gus Edwards of the Baltimore Ravens, who is currently the number one running back on the number one team in football, a league leader in touchdowns, and who followed his passion to the highest mountaintops of sports; or Matthew Caldwell, my best childhood friend who is now being recognized as one of the greatest executives in all of sports, and whose team, the Florida Panthers, just went to the Stanley Cup Finals; or Jason Marquis, a MLB all-star and World Series pitcher who is the best athlete I have ever seen in my life, and has not only been a role model for me throughout my life, but is a master of this reality to the likes that many of us can only dream of; or my first boss on Wall Street whose ability to communicate and lead men made him a billionaire, these individuals mastered this reality because they all followed *the Formula*.

The Formula is Bashar's masterpiece creation, as are many other valuable lessons previously mentioned in this book, and after I learned it, many questions I had about my past were answered.

Very simply, when was the last time you were excited for the next day to begin? When was the last time you couldn't wait to wake up in the morning and take on the day? For me, looking back, there were many more days of struggle than excitement in my life. *The Formula changes that because it unlocks one of the greatest secrets known to man—**the*** *idea that excitement isn't just a feeling; it's a roadmap, it's a path, it's a direction to your most fulfilling life, and when you act on it and you follow the synchronicities along the way, you will be led to your purpose, to your passion, to your greatest life, to your destiny!*

Once you apply the Formula, life will be your own fairy tale, but far from fiction, this formula will be a blueprint, an instruction manual that will help you become more of the real you, the true you, the you that has always been there waiting to emerge or reemerge in this lifetime. Let this formula be the key that opens the door to your most desired life. Let it be the compass pointing in the direction of the best you. Let it be the light when you are surrounded by darkness, or simply allow it to navigate when you are lost, but most importantly, let it guide you on a path that leads you to a wonderful life of bliss, happiness, joy, and fulfillment!

Are you ready to discover your true purpose in life? Are you ready to learn the formula?

"The Formula"—5 Simple Steps to Become the True You!

Step #1: Act on your highest excitement every moment you can.

Step #2: Take your passion and excitement as far as you can take it, until you can't take it any further.

Step #3: Act on your passion and excitement with absolutely zero insistence or assumption concerning a specific outcome.

Step #4: Remain in a positive state throughout the entire process and allow synchronicity to guide you.

Step #5: Examine your belief systems and let go of the fear-based ones.

<u>Step #1</u> of the Formula

Act on your highest excitement every moment you can.

The things in life that excite you aren't random. They are connected to your true purpose. Follow them! What is the most exciting thing you can think of doing right now? What is your passion? What drives you?

It doesn't have to be a long-term career or project; it can simply be something you'd like to do at this very moment that brings you joy. Perhaps you like to write, to sing, to play the piano, to run, to hike, to cook, to clean, to swim. If your passion is politics, then create a blog or a podcast, write a book, or if you feel daring, run for office. If your passion is dancing, then maybe by opening a dance studio you will fulfill your true purpose. Do you like sports? If so, go out and watch or play a sport; you never know who you'll run into—maybe it's someone who will change your life.

The idea is to allow the feelings of excitement and joy to help you discover what it is that you love to do, because once you follow your joy, synchronicities and coincidences will guide you to your next step! When you take a step in the direction of your excitement, you never know who you will meet along the way, you never know what inspiration may come to you, you never know what opportunities will find you when you are following your excitement.

Excitement has its own energetic system, and it will feed the body and mind with all the physical and mental energy needed to help keep you focused on your passion. That's why it's important to do what you love to do. If a person can stay in this blissful state, then they will continuously tap into this energy and, in many cases, accomplish what they thought was impossible. Even if you feel unmotivated or unenergetic at this very moment, when you take a step in the direction of your passion, the energy will find you!

> *Take action on whatever has more excitement in it than any other choice at any moment you can, no matter what level this is on. It's that simple. Here's how it works: if taking a walk on the beach is the most exciting thing you can do at the moment, then act on it. Who knows who you may meet on the way to the beach? Who knows what you might overhear? Who knows what you may see that will inspire you in some way that you wouldn't have been inspired if you went and done something less exciting.*
> **–Bashar**

Remember, be on the lookout for synchronicity and coincidences, as they will guide you throughout the entire process. The degree of synchronicities can range from viewing repeating numbers everywhere you look to witnessing bone-chilling coincidences that may freak you out in the beginning but become normal the more you follow the Formula.

Warning: **addiction does not constitute following your excitement.** When people are not feeding their creative spirit, when they're not leading their best life or becoming their true selves, they often seek escape with the use of chemically altering drugs or behaviors, such as sex or gambling. If you are at war with a choice, then most likely it's not the path you should follow.

Be mindful of the difference between excitement and anxiety or fear. Excitement powers itself and doesn't wear off until you are ready for it to wear off. Excitement will not trigger feelings of withdrawal or guilt; instead, it will generate feelings of joy and fulfillment. Excitement supports us mentally, physically, emotionally, and spiritually and will act as a road map directing us to our very next thread of excitement.

<u>Step #2</u> of the Formula

*Take your passion and excitement as far as you can take it,
until you can't take it any further.*

Greg Belson, a star baseball player in high school, went on to become
an all-American at Montclair State University and was drafted by
the Arizona Diamondbacks in the year 2000. Greg excelled in the
minor leagues, but injuries cut his career short. Baseball was his
excitement, and although his playing career was over, he never
left the game. All he did was transition to another aspect of his
excitement—instead of playing in the major leagues, he opened up
his own baseball training facility, where he would go on to help
many other players become stars.

Another childhood friend of mine, Brian Esposito, was drafted in
the major leagues in the year 2000. Brian had a lengthy professional
career, which included trips back and forth from the minors to the
majors while switching teams along the way. Although his playing
days came to an end, he too never left the game and is now in his 9th
year as a major league manager, currently in the San Diego Padre
farm system.

My next example is another tremendous athlete who I had the honor
to coach. His name is Zach Granite. Zach was a star baseball player,
but he also played basketball for me when I was a high school teacher
and a coach. An amazing athlete, Zach wound up being drafted by
the Minnesota Twins in 2013. After tearing up the minor leagues in
hitting, Zach finally got his chance to play in the majors. In his very
first game, he made one of the greatest plays of the year, robbing all-
star Manny Machado of what would have been a 3-run homer. Not
only did Zach excel in his first season, but he helped the Twins reach
the playoffs that year.

Zach, too, would suffer numerous injuries which ended his playing career, but he never left the game of baseball. Shortly after leaving the major leagues, he opened up his own baseball clinic and is now an athletic trainer specializing in baseball.

Injuries have a clever way of pulling us in a certain direction we otherwise would not have gone. They cause people to go within, allowing for the person to heal physically and often mentally and emotionally as well. Even something like an injury can be a gift from God because it seems that injuries are the Universe's way of pushing us—or sometimes ramming us—in a direction that is more compatible with our true purpose.

The stories of Greg, Brian, and Zach are long-term examples of the idea of following our excitement to the best of our ability while taking it as far as we can go, allowing synchronicity and coincidence to guide us step by step. I'll say it again: **a person who does what they love to do will never have to work a day in their life.** Do what you love to do just because you love to do it. Don't worry how it looks, because what excites you, does so for a reason!

Remember, our highest excitement does not need to be a long-term project or career move. It could be something as simple as reading a book, taking a nap, or simply walking in nature. Whatever excites you moment to moment is what you need to do. In the case of reading a book, you may read something that motivates you, inspires you, or sparks an idea that can actually lead you to your next thread of excitement. Maybe, during a nap, you dream of an idea, perhaps an invention that would make the world a better place and change the course of history. Maybe, while walking in nature, you find some kind of inspiration that moves you in a certain direction.

The higher mind, The Universe, and all of creation know exactly what we need, at the exact time we need it, not a second before but also, not a second later, so trust in it! If something excites you, it does so for a reason, a reason that may not be discovered until a later time.

*If you cannot see a way to act on a specific excitement at a specific moment in time, all you need to do is act on your next highest excitement that you are capable of acting on. Take it as a road sign directing you on a slightly different path. The path may wind back around to your original excitement, or it may put you on a much different path which could be even better than you initially imagined. –***Bashar**

Warning: if you don't act on an opportunity, you may not get a second chance. Don't let your fear block the path that leads to your best life! **Remember:** when you act on your excitement you will be guided from one step to the next by way of synchronicity and coincidence so ACT, ACT, ACT!

*Act on your excitement to the fullest degree you can act. If more than one opportunity has an equal ability to be acted upon, choose either one, then allow synchronicity to guide you down that path. Keep acting on it until you have no more ability to act. When you cannot act on it any further, choose the next most exciting thing you are able to take action on. Recognize the signs, reflections, and agreements that indicate an inability to take action. For example, physical parameters, societal laws, moral values, and ethical standards can all indicate whether or not you have the ability to take action. –***Bashar**

In my travels, I've discovered that many people like to hold on to beliefs such as, "To succeed, you have to sacrifice and struggle," or "To make it in life, you have to give up what you like to do in order to do what you need to do." I went through life thinking similarly.

But I was wrong! You don't have to give up anything. You don't have to struggle. You don't have to sacrifice. You don't have to do anything in this world you don't want to do, and instead, it would be advantageous to do whatever it is that you truly want to do because that's when the magic happens, that's when the Universe and all the synchronicities and coincidences make themselves known. Remember, your beliefs are always true, so if you BELIEVE that you have to sacrifice and struggle, then by all means, struggle away, don't let me stop you, but just know that your path of least resistance revolves around you doing what excites you in life and not the other way around.

Step #3 of the Formula

Act on your passion and excitement with absolutely zero insistence or assumption with respect to a specific outcome.

Before becoming a professional baseball player, an amateur pro golfer, and eventually, one of the most successful high school baseball coaches in NYC history, winning many city championships and coaching numerous professional athletes, my friend Tom Tierney Jr. would learn a lesson he'd never forget. Whenever Tom was at baseball practice, he would always see some kid playing racquetball, day after day, night after night, but he thought racquetball was nothing but a waste of time. He never knew why this kid loved playing that game so much, especially since "you couldn't get a scholarship or make any money from that sport professionally."

Tom, being one of the best athletes in NYC at the time, decided to get on the racquetball court and play this kid. He wanted to show the kid that he was wasting his time playing a "dead-end sport." The kid wound up beating Tom pretty badly, and the competitiveness in Tom came out in a tirade as he went off on the kid, telling him to his face that he was "wasting his time playing racquetball" and that he "would never make anything of himself playing this stupid sport." Little did Tom know that Sudsy Monchik would become the best racquetball player the world has ever seen, finishing five years as the #1 ranked racquetball player in the world from 1996–2001. In addition to his #1 ranking, Sudsy went on to win eleven Junior World Championship titles, four US Open titles, and six doubles titles, including the national doubles championship in 1994. If that's not enough, he also won gold medals for the United States at both the 1998 US Olympic Festival and the 1995 Pan American Games while earning millions of dollars throughout his career.

The moral of the story is that we should do what we love to do just because we love to do it and for no other reason. It's the person who plays because they love to play who will find the energy and focus to succeed long-term. As soon as we desire a specific outcome, like the need to get a scholarship or become a professional athlete, we put pressure on ourselves to perform, and we lose that magical energetic vibration that will help us succeed in the long term. The state of mind of expectation can lead to unnecessary stress and disappointment, which can eventually lead to failure.

When we let go of insistence on a specific outcome, we leave room for the Universe to potentially bring us an experience or an outcome more wonderful and more magical than we could ever have imagined ourselves. Our intentions could actually limit our potential, so the idea is to remain in a state of excitement and allow the Universe to produce for us the most preferable experience possible.

Insistence equals resistance! The reason it's crucial to drop any insistence about the outcome of acting on your passion is because our limited physical mind, in most cases, isn't capable of determining the best possible outcome, although most of us have been trained to think we know better. We have a physical mind, designed to explore the experience we call physical reality, and we also have a non-physical higher mind, designed to guide the physical mind through that physical experience. It's like the physical mind is in the middle of the forest while the higher mind is standing on top of a tree, able to see what direction we should go to get to our desired destination. The higher mind has a broader view of what lies ahead, while the physical mind can barely guess what's around the next corner. So, insisting on a specific outcome, manifestation, or path may actually prevent a better manifestation from coming to fruition. –**Bashar**

That's why if we're stuck in a boring job, in a boring life, in a boring relationship, the higher mind, creation, and the Universe will communicate to us the feelings of BOREDOM, of dissatisfaction, which will cause our body to create DIS-EASE. We are here to create, we are here to live an exciting, fulfilling life, and since creation wants to experience itself through our eyes, we will be doing a terrible disservice to live an average, boring life.

Once you're in an excited state of mind, don't be surprised if something else that needs to manifest in your life does so just because you followed your initial excitement. We need to leave room open in our planning to allow for the most incredible and amazing outcome possible, which can be accomplished by doing what we love to do simply because we love to do it and not because we need it to look a certain way.

<u>Step #4</u> of the Formula

*Remain in a positive state and allow synchronicity
to guide you throughout the entire process.*

A great childhood friend of mine loved playing hockey. Although making money was his first excitement, playing hockey was his second. While playing hockey, my friend broke his leg and was stuck in his house for months. When visiting my friend, I remember seeing to-do lists and goal sheets spread out all over his desk. You see, my friend used this time constructively, and while he was bedridden, he thought of different business ideas.

During this time, the grass in front of his house became overgrown, and since he couldn't move his leg, he needed to call a landscaper. Every landscaper he called was busy. The ones he contacted couldn't get to his house for weeks. Other landscapers charged a fortune for simply cutting the lawn. My friend had concluded that landscaping must be a lucrative business since he couldn't find anyone to cut his overgrown grass for weeks.

Unable to do much with a broken leg in a caste, he planned to learn everything he could about landscaping. Following this excitement, he created his own landscaping business, and within two years, he was one of the most successful landscapers in NYC and became a self-made millionaire in the process. Now he lives in Brazil while teams of landscapers run his business. Because he remained in a positive state of mind, the Universe conspired in my friend's favor, and he turned a bad situation into a lucrative opportunity.

I have learned that if something doesn't work out, it's probably for my own good. It took me many years to learn this, but this is how it all works! If there is one thing for you to take from this book, it should be the idea that a positive state of being will attract to you the people, opportunities, and experiences that will make life worth living!

You can't truly master Step #4 of the Formula until you've mastered Step #3, which is to let go of any insistence on a specific outcome. As soon as you put conditions on your excitement or when you allow doubt to creep into your mind, such as, "If I don't make it to the major leagues, I will quit baseball," or "If I don't make it to Broadway, I am a failure," you take yourself out of the excited state, and with that, you may have a tough time attracting your dream scenario. As we have previously said, a life filled with doubt, worry, or any other negative fear-based emotion increases your chances of that reality coming to fruition.

Even if your life has been hell, as mine so often was, the Universe is conspiring in your favor, and you must constantly give thanks and trust. When things turn around, and they always do, it's the periods of hell that you persevered through that you'll remember the most because it's those experiences that made you the person you are today.

Have you ever had someone break up with you? At the time you thought your life was over, but within time, you wound up finding someone better and more compatible. Or maybe you were let go from a job only to find your dream job. Our limited physical mind cannot fathom what the Universe has in store for us, but if we just put our trust in it, everything else will work out. As long as you stay in a positive state and respond to circumstances in a positive way, things will ultimately work out in a way that's beneficial to you. So, we don't need to stress, we don't need to despair, we just need to relax. Remain in a positive state. Whenever we "lose something," it offers us the chance to find something better. Therefore, losses aren't endings; they are actually beginnings!

> *Discovering that which you don't prefer still counts as progress, because if you're still reacting negatively to situations on the basis of how things look, instead of responding from a positive state, despite appearances, then you haven't actually changed, and thus, the manifestation can only reflect disappointment.* **–Bashar**

Step #5 of the Formula

Examine your belief systems and let go of any fear-based beliefs.

This may take practice, but as soon as you truly let go of the thoughts and beliefs that hold you back, you will have cracked a secret code solved by the most successful and influential people throughout history.

> *You change fear-based beliefs by first discovering what they are, and the way you go about doing that in any given situation when you find yourself reacting emotionally in a way that you don't prefer is just to have a conversation with yourself. You must ask yourself, "If I actually chose to be the person I prefer to be, what am I most terrified might happen?" That will usually reveal to you the fear-based belief holding you back.* **–Bashar**

Even the greatest of persons at some point in their life will encounter what I would refer to as the doubt monster! You know—the "I'm not good enough," "I'm not worthy," "Everyone will laugh at me" thoughts we have on our path to greatness. To overcome these moments of unnecessary fear and worry, great people fully trust in their own self-worth, and they call upon this confidence and inner strength whenever they need to slay the invisible evil force of doubt! Great people do not settle for mediocrity. They know that the comfort zone is where greatness goes to die! Therefore, they do not fear the unknown because the pain of living an unexciting unremarkable life overcomes their fear of failure, and whatever challenge is thrown at them along the way, they know they'll be able to figure it out. Not because they're better than everyone else. It's because these people have already done it before, and in doing so, they have become their own *guides of greatness*.

So, it's imperative to constantly investigate your belief systems and remove and replace beliefs that are unpreferred. My belief when writing this book was that since I was a terrible writer all throughout high school, college, and graduate school, I figured there was no way I was going to be able to write a book; however, the more I wrote, the easier it got. Then I figured it was probably going to cost a fortune to publish this book, until the CEO of Bashar Communications, April Rochelle, pointed me to a publisher that was a fraction of the price. Then I figured it would cost a fortune to market this book. That's until I was led to certain people who knew exactly what to do, and they were able to direct me throughout the entire process free of charge. I no longer allow any limitation or negative belief to stop me from my desired outcome. Let this book serve as proof and testament that any negative belief can be overturned, transformed, or redefined to serve you in the most beneficial and advantageous way.

Pursuing Multiple Excitements

There was a young kid who had a passion for singing. While in his early teens, he auditioned for the play *Wicked* and got a lead part, but although theater offered this young man the chance to act and perform on stage, his drive to sing pulled him in a slightly different direction. He courageously quit *Wicked* so that he could try out for *American Idol*.

He barely made it past Simon Cowell in the first live audition, but one thing led to another, and Adam Lambert earned second place on the show and a reputation as one of the best performers in the history of *American Idol*. Now, second place for some would've been heartbreaking, but for Lambert, it worked out even better. Without being totally tied up in the *American Idol* contract, Lambert was free to flourish on his own. And that's exactly what he did.

Even though performing in plays was exciting, it wasn't Adam Lambert's highest excitement, but it did lead him to eventually becoming one of the top singer/songwriters in the world, selling over 3M albums and 5M singles in the process. Lambert became so successful that the legendary band Queen invited him to perform with them on a world tour, and the rest is history.

> *If you have multiple passions with a similar level of excitement, you can act on them to whatever degree you can act on those different expressions, according to how synchronicity brings them to you. You can also take turns, acting on them according to whatever your preference is at that current moment. If you are stuck between two different passions, you can even flip a coin.* –**Bashar**

That's exactly what Bashar told me to do when I told him that I was confused about whether or not I should move to New Jersey or Florida. Bashar said, "Adam, flip a coin." I told him I was nervous to flip a coin, because what if it landed on Florida? He said, "You see, you got your answer."

Deep down, I was too nervous to move to Florida, and by just *thinking* about flipping a coin, I was able to discover some favorability in the idea of moving to New Jersey. I didn't even have to flip the coin, because the idea of wanting the coin to land a certain way—which in this case was New Jersey—told me everything I needed to know about my motivations.

> *Excitement is the thread that's connected to all other expressions of excitement in your life, and it will be the path of least resistance as you follow it. It will activate all other expressions of that excitement in whatever form they may come in your life, and even though some things that excite you now may look very different than the things that excited you in your so-called past, just go by the level of excitement. That is the real you, your true vibration, the vibration of love, the feeling of Christmas morning, or whatever exciting celebratory event that fills you with ecstatic uncontrollable joy, that gives you goosebumps and a warm feeling all through the body. The "real you" is the actual state of excitement and unconditional love.* **–Bashar**

In Conclusion

As you have already learned, we are not alone in this life—hidden from our immediate perception is a mysterious force that seems to be connected to all things. If we follow "the Formula" and allow the synchronicities to guide us, we will eventually be led to our true purpose in life and this once imperceptible force now becomes direct proof that a divinely orchestrated intelligence exists! The best part is just by doing what we love to do from one moment to the next we activate this force and all the magic that comes with it.

When we do what excites us or when we tap into our creative energy force we will be guided by way of synchronicity and coincidence so that, not only do we follow the correct path, but we become the path itself offering those who know us the opportunity to follow our example. By creating, we take control of our destiny, and outside forces will no longer have the control over us that they had in the past.

Just the journey alone in discovering *"our passion"* can be one of the most exhilarating, uplifting, and fulfilling experiences life has to offer. So, let the excitement of possibility energize you, allow the opportunity for your creativity to flourish, and be mindful of the synchronistic and serendipitous moments, as they may appear as plentiful as the air we breathe. Be that person you were born to be, do what you love to do, stay in a positive state during this entire process, and appreciate this co-creation we call life!

Action Plan
Bashar's Intention Activation

The solar plexus located at the bottom of the breastplate is the chakra point of intention. When you get excited about something you feel that energy in the pit of your stomach. That vibration in the solar plexus that gets your juices flowing, that feeling of certitude, the feeling of certainty, that knowingness that this is right for you. Filtering that energy through negative belief systems is called anxiety.

That's why you also get that feeling of butterflies in the pit of your stomach. What we call butterflies in the stomach is the chakra of intention, and when it manifests itself as anxiety in the pit of your stomach, it tells you that you're activating your energy of your intention, but you're filtering them through negative beliefs. When you allow yourself to know that's the activation vibration, the emotion (Energy + Motion = Emotion) in the chakra of intention, then you can allow it to manifest as that scintillating excitement that you feel as a child when it is about to do something exciting, when it knows something exciting is on its way. It's the feeling that you get when it is about to be Christmas morning or Hanukkah or whatever celebratory event that excites you.

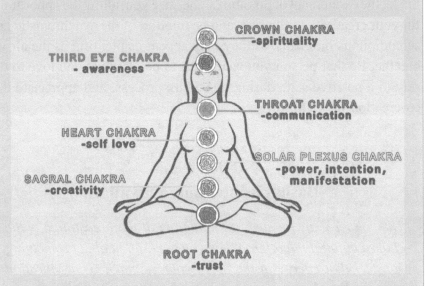

Intention is the idea of knowing that you are about to open a present of more of yourself. If you allow yourself to imagine yourself in that ideal scenario, and not just the point of view of it, but see that version of you in that scenario, like you're looking in a mirror. The idea is to see what that version of you is doing in that scenario. How that version of you is behaving in that scenario, and regardless of whether that scenario exists, you know that that version of you would behave similarly no matter what's going on in their reality.

Once you have created the image of yourself in that scenario, allow that image of you to face you literally while looking into a mirror. But in looking into that mirror, you can see that all the representations of the reality of that version of you are representations of that reality and do not necessarily reflect what's going on in this reality. You can see the difference between the two. The idea is to really pay attention to how you are looking in that reality, how you are behaving, look at your body language, look at your attitude. Feel your attitude and how it's different perhaps from the attitude, body language, energy, or feelings you are having right now as you create that scenario.

When you have in that picture of your ideal scenario, whatever the best representation of your imagination your physical mind can conjure at that moment, allow yourself then to add this into the picture, to see a beam of laser light going from your solar plexus to the solar plexus of the reflection in that reality. See this connection and feel this connection with power and intention. Feel that connection, feel that chord, that unbreakable chord between you.

You are now connected to this vibration and all the information that you need is coming from that version of you, from that chord filling up your solar plexus, rewiring you, programming you, reinventing you, redefining you, filling you up with all the necessary data that you can decide to incorporate in your being to become that version of you. To become one with that version. Allow yourself to feel that exchange of energy, that exchange of information, that powerful vibrating humming, and that stabbing beam of laser-like light from solar plexus to solar plexus.

Feel it cooling you down, heating you, however you wish to feel it in your imagination. It doesn't matter, just know you are receiving the appropriate information that you choose to allow to download into your matrix to rewire your brain, rewire your neurology, reengineer your DNA, rearrange your molecular structure, rearrange the vibration you are giving off in your current reality. Then allow yourself to imagine at that point that everything here in this reality is starting to morph to everything in that reality until such time that the two images match as perfect reflections of one another. When they click, when they match, when they vibrate in harmony, you will then imagine that they are humming and vibrating like tuning forks, like two mirrors facing each other vibrating. And as that frequency is amplified along that laser-like light connecting your solar plexus, it becomes one overwhelming tone that permeates and penetrates every cell of your body, every single image within those reflections, until everything is singing that song. Take a deep breath in and sigh! Let yourself relax with that idea.

You'll be putting out with that laser light, a specific frequency that eventually your reality will collapse onto until the whole vibration of your entire reality is exactly that frequency, and nothing, nothing, nothing can happen that doesn't happen within that frequency. From that point forward, there will be no soft focus in a sense, there will be no opportunity for any other choice to be made for any other frequency to come in because you are not choosing anything else but what, you know, falls into the frequency of that laser light of intention coming from your solar plexus. That's your beacon, that's your searchlight, that's your light, that's your path, that's your frequency, that's you!

Conclusion

How did it come to this?

One moment this man was trying out for a spot on the Green Bay Packers football team, the next he was bagging groceries at $5.50 an hour at the local supermarket. And just like that, his dream of playing professional football was over.

It really wasn't much of a dream to begin with. Any college player can apply for an NFL tryout, more of a courtesy offered to graduates than a serious consideration. Besides, he was competing against one of the greatest players to ever play the game: Brett Favre.

When the young man took the field, he was so scared and so unprepared, that he hesitated to go on the field and was cut before he could even throw a pass.

What was he thinking? He knew he couldn't play football professionally. He was a backup quarterback for most of his high school career. He didn't get any scholarship offers when he graduated high school, and if it wasn't for the young man sending his own highlight tapes to local colleges, a task usually performed by a coach or a college scout, the kid would have never earned a spot on his local college football team. Even though he was able to sliver his way onto his local college football team in small-town Iowa, he didn't play until his fifth and final year. What would make him think he could play in the National Football League?

Even though football didn't work out, this young man was grateful he still had his job at the local supermarket. A small part of this man knew if he ever had another chance to prove himself again on the field, he wouldn't fail. Perhaps the thought of stocking shelves for the rest of his life was the exact motivation this man needed to overcome his fear of playing quarterback professionally.

Unfortunately, it would take the miracle of all miracles for this man to ever play quarterback professionally, but as we have said so often in this book, with the right attitude and the understanding that there is a force that operates beyond our vision, beyond our purview, carefully orchestrating the best-case scenario for those able to tap into it, *miracles become the norm in life, not the exception.*

Miraculously, out of all the places in the world for a professional football team to spring up, the Arena Football League chose Iowa to be the home to its newest franchise. Although the Arena Football League was far from the glitz and glam of the National Football League, it was still a professional franchise, nonetheless. With the season ready to begin and in desperate need of a quarterback the Iowa Barnstormers' frantic search led them in the direction of a local kid who barely played in high school, who sat on the bench most of his college career, who was passed up by every team in the NFL draft, and who was now bagging groceries at the HYVEE supermarket not far from the arena.

Not knowing what to expect but putting his faith in a higher power, **Kurt Warner** agreed to play for the Barnstormers, and just like that the greatest Cinderella story in the history of sports was about to begin. It was at this time that Warner believed *the Universe was conspiring in his favor.*

Although the AFL was more of an out-of-control men's league that paid very little money and offered little safety from injury, it was more lucrative than working for minimum wage at a supermarket, and who knows? If he played well enough, maybe he'd get a call from an NFL team.

The Arena Football League allowed Warner to continue his excitement of playing football, and this time he would take it as far as he could take it, until he couldn't take it any further. What were the odds that an expansion football team would pop up out of nowhere in Iowa and just so happen to be looking for a quarterback? He didn't know how to explain it, but he just knew things were working out in his favor. Once Warner tapped into this cosmic force, there was very little that could stop him, and just like that, this miracle man would go from grocery store worker to one of the best players in Arena Football League history, breaking many records along the way.

But this story far from over!

After three years playing in the Arena Football League, he got a call from the St. Louis Rams of the NFL. The old Kurt Warner was scared to death to play in the NFL, but the new Kurt Warner believed in a higher power; he believed in not only himself but the fact that the Universe seemed to be paving a path toward something magical. *Circumstances no longer mattered* to Kurt. He knew he would arise to any occasion, so when the highly touted quarterback Trent Green, then the starter of the St. Louis Rams, got injured before the season began, Kurt Warner would go from grocery store worker to AFL star to NFL starter.

With no fear and a deep trust in a higher power, Kurt Warner would achieve the impossible, taking the St. Louis Rams to the Super Bowl where he would lead his team to the championship. To add to the miracle season, Kurt would take home Super Bowl MVP and MVP of the entire league, a feat accomplished by only a handful of players throughout history.

Kurt would go on to appear in two more Super Bowls, he would win one more MVP, and after twelve magical seasons in the NFL, he would make the Hall of Fame where he'd be remembered forever in the annals of time as one of the greatest players in NFL history.

Looking back, if Kurt hadn't taken action and sent his own VHS highlight tapes to local colleges, he never would have gotten a partial scholarship to Northern Iowa. If he hadn't stayed in a good frame of mind throughout college while he sat on the bench for most of it, he never would have played in his senior year. If he hadn't continued following his excitement by playing in the Arena Football League, he never would have had the opportunity to play in the NFL, and if talented starting quarterback Trent Green hadn't gotten hurt playing in that preseason game for the Rams, Kurt may never have seen the field in the NFL. You see, Kurt Warner followed the synchronicities and was led to greatness.

Those who believe in miracles and who realize the universe is conspiring in their favor create the very miracles they believe in. Those who understand that circumstances in life don't matter and who, by acting on their excitement, take full advantage of the power of momentum and go on to achieve the impossible. Those who are grateful for all they encounter on their journey and who remain positive throughout the entire process form around them an invincible force field of power and greatness, impenetrable by the limitations set forth by all Matrix systems.

No matter how many times people count them out, no matter how many times they fall, stumble, and get knocked down, great people never quit, and like alchemists, magicians, or wizards, they bend the will of the world in whatever direction they see fit! It is they who shatter beliefs; it is they who shatter Matrix programming; it is they who achieve the impossible; it is they who show the rest of us what's possible!

The Seven Secrets

Secret #1: Miracles are the Norm—We often think miracles are rare and are magical occurrences, but miracles are not the exception to the rule; they are the true natural order of things. The most successful people throughout history have figured this out. **The goal of Secret #1 is to recognize that this miracle force exists, tap into this magic, and allow the coincidences and synchronicities to guide you in the direction of your greatest self.**

Secret #2: Circumstances Don't Matter—The state of being we are in determines what we attract in our lives. Everything we have, everything we do, everything we are, everything we will be is determined by our state of being—which is the sum of our thoughts, feelings, beliefs, and actions. **This is Secret #2: circumstances in life don't matter; it's our state of being that does. If we constantly focus on the emotions of pain, frustration, lack of abundance, and struggle, we amplify these energies and run the risk of attracting negative experiences that mirror our negative emotional state. On the other hand, if we focus and take action on the things that excite us, that make us healthier, that are more representative of our best and truest selves, we will attract more positive experiences that mirror our positive emotional state.** You'll know your state of being has changed when you no longer react negatively to circumstances. When you control your reactions, you control your life!

Secret #3: The Universe Conspires in Our Favor—If you want to get the Universe on your side, you need to realize that **the Universe is already on your side!** Even if the experience did not seem pleasant at the time, you need to understand that it was the very experience you needed to have in your life to help you learn, grow, and become the true you. **The goal of Secret #3 is to know that the Universe is and has always been conspiring in our favor, and no matter how bad an experience may seem initially, give it time because you may just find out that a past or present nightmare is a future blessing.**

Secret #4: The Power of Momentum—**The goal of Secret #4 is that by taking bold action in the direction of your dream or your passion, you initiate the power of momentum.** Even one small step in the direction of your passion will suffice because once momentum is activated, the energy generated from getting the ball rolling will take on a life of its own and propel you forward, without you having to do much more than just remain in an excited and positive state throughout the entire process.

Secret #5: Gratefulness is the Vibration of Greatness—Being grateful is the one gift we can give the Universe, and as soon as we show gratitude, the Universe seems to find a way to give us more to be grateful for. **This is Secret #5: the idea that an invisible power that guides all things waits for us to be grateful for what we already have to provide us with more of what we desire.** Think about that! Would you rather give a gift to someone who's appreciative or a person who couldn't care less? Do you believe the Universe to be any different?

Secret #6: The Journey is the Destination—You have heard the saying, "If you don't know where you're going, how will you know when you get there?" Many people look for a final destination point in their journey, but once that point is reached, they somehow seem unfulfilled and look for another destination point. **Secret #6 is the idea that the journey is the destination, the path is the process, the experience itself is the goal, and wisdom gained is the gift.** While on your journey, just know that all the good stuff, all the bad, all the highs, all the lows help guide us and help mold us so that we can become the best us, the true us, the wise us, the great us!

Secret #7: "The Formula"—5 Simple Steps to Become the True You!

Step #1: Act on your highest excitement every moment you can.

The things in life that excite you aren't random. They are connected to your true purpose. Follow them! What is the most exciting thing you can think of doing right now? What is your passion? What drives you? The self-reflection, self-awareness, and the journey of discovering our passion is one of the greatest gifts for the soul!

Step #2: Take your passion and excitement as far as you can take it until you can't take it any further.

If you cannot see a way to act on a specific excitement at a specific moment in time, all you need to do is act on your next highest excitement that you can act on. Take it as a road sign directing you on a slightly different path. The path may wind back around to your original excitement, or it may put you on a much different path, which could be even better than you imagined.

Step #3: Act on your passion and excitement with absolutely zero insistence or assumption for a specific outcome.

There's nothing wrong with desiring a specific outcome, like the need to get a scholarship or become a professional athlete, but when we put immense pressure on ourselves to reach a certain level of achievement, we run the risk of losing that magical, carefree, energetic vibration that will help us succeed in the long term. Expectations can lead to unnecessary stress and disappointment, which can eventually lead to burnout and failure. The idea is to feel the feeling of the most exciting outcome you can imagine, then operate in that vibration while you're practicing, while you're performing, while you're engulfed in your passion because in doing so, nothing at all can stop you from accomplishing feats you previously thought were unattainable.

You may lose. You may fail. You may be laughed at, and many will doubt you, but if you remain in the vibration of excitement regardless of outside circumstances, regardless of others' expectations of you, then eventually, everything and everyone will have no choice but to move aside to make room for your greatness. There is no expiration point for greatness, so when you do what you love without expectation, eventually, you will reach a certain level of greatness or be led to something even greater.

Step #4: Remain in a positive state and allow synchronicity to guide you throughout the entire process.

If doubt or worry creeps into your mind, so what? Think of it as an opportunity to prove yourself to the Universe that you are mentally strong and deserving of all the wonder, joy, excitement, and greatness your passion has to offer. Taking action is the mortal enemy of worry, doubt, and fear, so whenever you're feeling down, act!

When we do what excites us and when we tap into our creative energy force we will be guided by way of synchronicity and coincidence so that, not only do we follow the correct path, but we become the path itself. By creating, we take control of our destiny, and outside forces will no longer have the control over us that they had in the past.

Step #5: Investigate your belief systems and remove and replace fear-based beliefs.

These beliefs appear in the form of unnecessary doubts and worries. You know, the "I'm not good enough," or "People will think I'm nuts" fear-based beliefs that hold us back from becoming the greatest person we could be. When this happens, you just have to ask yourself, "What am I afraid will happen if I become the person I'm truly meant to be?" This will usually reveal the fear-based belief out of alignment, and once you discover the belief, it no longer becomes a belief; it becomes a choice.

The best part is, you get to choose what you want to believe in life! As Bashar says, "It's that simple, unless you want to complicate things."

The best part about all the Secrets you have learned in this book is the fact that you don't necessarily have to do anything different in your life. You don't need to work harder; you don't need to earn more money; you don't need to do anything but be more of your true self. Just do what you want to do in this life and not what you think others want you to do.

Do you have to apply all the Secrets in this book to create your dream life? Not at all. In fact, if you just follow the Formula, you will automatically apply many of the secrets learned in this book. That's the beauty of the Seven Secrets—each Secret is so powerful and so magical that any one Secret can help you bend the will of the world in whatever direction you want it to bend.

So, if we sit down to write a book, or write a song, or write a screenplay, we don't have to worry, we don't have to overthink, we don't have to over plan, or wonder, "Where in the world do we begin?" The answers will come! We will find the words, we will get in the rhythm, we will create the momentum, and as soon as we act, the Universe will guide us by way of coincidence and synchronicity, and with that, we will be guided every step along the way.

Everything that exists is part of creation. We are born to create. We exist to create. What we create we add to creation. What we add to creation we add to existence. And what we add to existence can echo in eternity.

What can you create? Remember, no one in the world is like you. You are unique, so what you can share with the world is an experience like no other. Each one of us is born with certain talents and abilities, and the Universe is screaming for us to share these abilities with the rest of the world. So, if you're a college student, working a 9–5 job, unemployed, or a housewife, find time to create something that represents the true you. Your unique gifts are waiting to be received.

About The Author

A dam Yannotta is a seasoned finance professional, thriving real estate investor, and former teacher operating in the New York metropolitan area. Graduating with a degree in finance, Adam entered the high-pressure world of Wall Street, where he learned invaluable lessons in managing money and thriving in challenging environments. His success in finance allowed him to retire before the age of forty and venture into real estate and other businesses.

Adam's unique journey led him to become a dedicated teacher, where he saw the flaws in the education system and worked diligently to improve it. He organized health programs and introduced various programs in sports medicine, nutrition, anatomy, and exercise physiology, inspiring countless students to pursue careers in the health field. As an educator, he excelled, earning advanced degrees in education and leadership.

In his book, *The Seven Secrets of Greatness: How to Discover Your Purpose, Find Your Power & Achieve the Impossible*, Adam shares his life's philosophy and beliefs, backed by his personal experiences and mathematical principles. This book is the culmination of his knowledge, including insights from his interactions with some of the most brilliant minds, athletes, and spiritual advisors that he has had the opportunity to meet and learn from. Adam's dedication to helping others and his commitment to fulfilling lives shine through in his work, offering readers a transformative journey towards abundance, gratitude, and the limitless potential of greatness.

Adam's passion extends beyond his writing, as he enjoys a daily routine filled with learning new skills, playing musical instruments, and providing anonymous acts of kindness to those in need. His fulfilling family life, coupled with his commitment to self-improvement and helping others, embodies the essence of his book's teachings.

Endnotes

i   Jeannine Lemare Calaba, *First Documentary*.

ii

iii

iv www.qz.com.

v   Rhonda Byrne, "The Secret."

vi Matt Frazier, www.nomeathlete.com

vii

viii *Missing Links, episode 7.*

ix

x   Deion Sanders.

xi

xii

xiii Stephen Covey, *The 7 Habits of Highly Effective People.*

xiv www.artofmanliness.com.

Made in United States
Cleveland, OH
05 February 2025

14108873R00085